ON THE CLOCK: DALLAS COWBOYS

ON THE CLOCK: DALLAS COWBOYS

Behind the Scenes with the Dallas Cowboys at the NFL Draft

CALVIN WATKINS

TRIUMPH
BOOKS

Library of Congress Cataloging-in-Publication Data available upon request.

This book is available in quantity at special discounts for your group or organization. For further information, contact:

Triumph Books LLC
814 North Franklin Street
Chicago, Illinois 60610
(312) 337-0747
www.triumphbooks.com

Printed in U.S.A.
ISBN: 978-1-63727-130-8
Design by Preston Pisellini
Page production by Patricia Frey
Photos courtesy of AP Images

To my family, all of them, particularly Cindy, who had to listen to me rant and rave about writing and reporting and just being a knucklehead. I love her very much, and without her and my family, this wouldn't be possible.

CONTENTS

FOREWORD

DRAFT **DAY IN** 1981 was very disappointing. There were 12 rounds back then. I never expected to hear my name early because I'm a realistic person. I know people now look at Grambling State University in a different light, but when it got down to about the sixth round and I saw that they were picking six other cornerbacks and safeties, I was surprised.

I went to my accounting class during the draft. And before I even came back from class, the Dallas Cowboys—along with the Buffalo Bills and New Orleans Saints—were already on campus and holding a three-month contract. The sixth round wasn't over yet, and they already had their minds made up. That pissed me off because it shows I never had a chance to get drafted. I was 21 years old. I just had led the nation in interceptions. But I figured I'd make the best of not getting drafted. At least I had a few choices unlike people who were getting drafted. The Cowboys secondary was horrible. I felt real comfortable going there and getting playing time. Plus, it's home. When you don't get drafted, then you really have to take advantage of each situation that comes your way and you have to be strategic. The Cowboys were a good fit because they were a winning organization who also had a need.

I knew wherever I went I had to make some things happen fast. My reaction was a sense of urgency. I never looked back. I don't know how many interceptions I got in training camp as a Cowboys rookie. I had three interceptions in the preseason. I had to take advantage of all those situations, and no receiver was going to beat me. That's how I felt. Before the draft former Oakland Raiders player and coach Willie Brown worked me out. I thought the Raiders wanted me. They didn't. It's okay.

I respect players who got drafted. Their stories are great. But people will always look at you as an undrafted player, no matter what you do. But getting drafted or not shouldn't stop your dream. I ended up getting to play for America's Team for nine years. I would later win a Super Bowl ring with the New York Giants. Bill Parcells was my coach there. He later coached the Cowboys, and some of his stories from the Cowboys' war room are featured here.

Not everyone gets drafted. Some of the greatest players in NFL history went undrafted. When you think about the Cowboys, some of the greatest players in franchise history didn't have their name called by an NFL commissioner welcoming them into the league. Drew Pearson was never drafted. That didn't stop him from being selected for the Pro Football Hall of Fame. I played 14 seasons in the NFL and held the Cowboys record for most interceptions in a single season at 11 until Trevon Diggs tied it during the 2021 season.

But I have an appreciation for the men who were drafted because I know how difficult it is to reach the National Football League. And the process behind the team's decisions aren't always straightforward. There is no better person to take you into the war room and behind those decisions than Calvin Watkins, a longtime respected beat reporter with *The Dallas Morning News.* There are always twists and turns when your team selects—or passes on—your favorite player. Here are their draft day stories.

—Everson Walls
Dallas Cowboys, 1981–89
Four-time Pro Bowler

INTRODUCTION

I HATE THE NFL draft.

Well, not anymore. But I used to.

It started early in the 2006 season when I was first placed on the Dallas Cowboys beat at *The Dallas Morning News*. My job was to cover the beat and attend home and away games and postseason events like the Senior Bowl and NFL Scouting Combine.

The Senior Bowl is the unofficial start of the NFL draft season. The first time I went—in the late winter of 2007 in Mobile, Alabama—coach Bill Parcells wasn't there, the Cowboys owner and general manager Jerry Jones wasn't there, and the scouts that attended were scared to speak with me. Parcells would retire soon thereafter, and then Wade Phillips took over.

I didn't really understand the draft. Yes, NFL teams draft players, but I always believed the play during the regular-season games was dismissed by coaches because they valued seeing the players at the Combine, Pro Days, and private workouts more than anything else. Scouts were devalued in my opinion because a head coach is judged on how the talent performs on the field.

But the draft picks themselves all have unique stories of how they got drafted. It doesn't matter what round. It doesn't matter what team. The fact you were part of a small fraternity means something. Getting drafted by an NFL team is an event nobody can take from a player. It's a cherished moment between family and friends, teammates, and anybody else who had even a sliver of impact in their life as an athlete. Over the years I've grown to appreciate the stories of the players and how and why they became drafted.

Those stories are a major reason why I changed my mind about the draft. The NFL draft is not so much about the players getting drafted but the families. It's about the dads who ran routes with their sons. It's about the moms who yelled from the sidelines as their sons played youth football. It's about the uncles and aunts and brothers and grandparents who sat on cold bleachers in November and December to watch high school football games. It's about a draft party. It's about having 15 to 20 people at the house or a hotel suite waiting for a phone call. It's a team of people living the dream with one player. It doesn't matter if it's the first or second round. It could be the seventh round. Everyone wants that call. Everyone wants to be wanted. That's what makes the draft so special. Sure, the scouts and personnel people have their say, but in reality the players dictate where they're getting drafted, and their stories of just getting to the point of receiving a draftable grade mean everything.

The scouts better get it right. In reality, trusting scouts is the lifeblood of any draft process. The men and women, who travel across the country to scout players and talk to their coaches, teammates, school employees about them, are vital to any evaluation of a prospective draft pick.

After years of covering the NFL, the draft is no longer an irritant on my skin. Sure, the process is maddening because you really don't know what a team is going to do until they make that final decision. But after close to 20 years covering the NFL, the NFL draft has become fun for me. It's an enjoyable experience, and I hope this book—whether you know some of these stories or not—will give you more of an appreciation of the people who were drafted by the Cowboys and the men and women who made those decisions.

1

ROGER STAUBACH

THE TOLL OF trying to win a championship wore on Don Meredith. The Dallas Cowboys quarterback was a great leader, the first true star in the history of the Cowboys.

He was nearly perfect for the job.

He was from East Texas—born and raised in a small town called Mount Vernon. If you looked for Meredith's childhood home, you could find it. Meredith was a Texas boy. He played high school football in Mount Vernon, college at Southern Methodist University, and just before his college career was over, he was going to play for the Cowboys. Everything he learned about football was on the fields of Texas. It was a true Texas/Hollywood story. East Texas kid plays college and pro ball locally.

All he had to do was win a championship in the pros.

Meredith had the temperament for it. The skill set, too. His coach, the legendary Tom Landry, was hard on him. The two survived on respect and friction. Landry wanted the offense run a certain way, and Meredith went with it. Sometimes. Meredith bore the brunt of increased expectations in the late 1960s, as the Cowboys went from expansion franchise to one of the elite teams in the NFL. But as the years dragged, Meredith couldn't push the franchise to the next level.

The burden on Meredith was tremendous. The criticism—fair or unfair—was something he held deep inside. He believed in his team. He believed in the city he played for. He believed in himself. Ultimately, it doesn't matter your feelings. A franchise must play the games on the field and win the games that count. That's all that matters.

Football was never a one-man game. Boxing. Tennis. Golf. Those are one-man sports, where despite the support system, it's the individual in the ring, golf course, or court that decides it. Yet in one of the ultimate team sports, the head coach and the quarterback have won-loss records. It's not fair. It's not right. It's just how the game is.

Meredith dealt with it.

Before the Cowboys turned themselves into an elite franchise whose draft picks finally turned into reliable players, the road was bumpy. No road to a title is smooth. Every championship run has obstacles meant to knock you off. The strongest teams sometimes don't win these titles. Luck can win a title. An injury to a key player on a better team can derail a championship run. A little mistake can disrupt a title appearance. Coaches and players tell you this builds a resolve in a team, especially the championship-level type of team Landry was trying to form.

In early December 1963, the Cowboys were in the midst of finishing a terrible season. It's part of that road a team takes to find greatness. Dallas held a 3–9 record, coming off a 34–27 loss to the New York Giants. With two games remaining in the regular season, it was time for the NFL draft. Back in the early stages of the NFL draft, it was held in the late part of the season. So officially the 1964 NFL Draft was held in 1963.

Part of building any team—no matter the sport—is a front office's ability to get new talent via draft selections. It's vital. The Cowboys were trying to morph from an expansion franchise to a title contender. The biggest way of changing your fortunes was the NFL draft.

The only way.

Coach Landry and general manager Tex Schramm were in Dallas making phone calls with their scouts and going over computerized scouting reports. Gil Brandt, the executive vice president of player personnel; Jack Eskridge, the equipment manager; and Larry Karl, the publicity director, were in Chicago. Back in the 1960s, the NFL draft wasn't conducted in New York at Radio City Music Hall or Madison Square Garden. The early stages of the NFL draft were held in hotel ballrooms in Chicago, Philadelphia, and New York. Team executives sat at round tables smoking cigarettes and cigars while waiting by the phone to be told who to select. The Cowboys were good at the gamesmanship of the NFL draft. Brandt understood this better than anybody. Brandt said the Cowboys would try to fake out teams about possible trades that would never happen. The small quarters, where these teams sat a few feet from each other, created rumors or truths about what a team might or might not do.

Brandt said he would leave the room with other executives to speak about trades. Sometimes he would head to the hotel lobby and make long-distance calls to Dallas and have Schramm and Landry on the line about trading with other teams. There were no time limits on these decisions, just decisions that needed making.

If a trade was to occur, Brandt would just get up from his seat and find another executive. Every team was watching each other. If a team executive stood up, *where was he going? Who was he talking to? What were they talking about?*

It was how things were done.

One great thing about the Cowboys was their vision. They just knew how to find players—whether it was at Historically Black Colleges, small schools, or the big schools. The Cowboys were a franchise wanting more than expansion labels. The Cowboys wanted an elite label. Brandt was in charge of finding the talent.

With an unlimited expense account, he knew it allowed him to travel to find players in different parts of the country. He didn't need to just seek players at the traditional big schools like Notre Dame, USC, Texas, and Oklahoma. Brandt would go west to Oregon. He would go to the Deep South talk with coach Eddie Robinson at Grambling State. He could travel to military academies to find players. That is what you did. That is what you had to do.

With so much information, the Cowboys could take their time with their selections. Of course, they weren't alone in this area. On December 2, 1963, with two games remaining in the regular season on a light snowy day in Chicago, the Cowboys were ready to improve their franchise. No different than anybody else.

It was a 20-round draft, and the Cowboys had 20 draft selections. In the previous year, the Cowboys selected 15 players with linebacker Lee Roy Jordan becoming their first-round pick. Dallas had traded five of its first 10 draft picks that season. Overall, the Cowboys selected 15 players. Trading was in Brandt's and Schramm's blood. Dallas was the first NFL team to utilize a computer to help evaluate talent. It was a complex formula that made the franchise revolutionary. In the eyes of some NFL teams, it made them look crazy. Green Bay Packers coach Vince Lombardi would joke about the draft cards the Cowboys held onto like cash. Those draft cards had information on the players that they would input into the computer. It would give them a grade on such a player, and the Cowboys would go from there. It wasn't the No. 1 thing that determined a draft pick but was part of the process.

The Cowboys didn't care what people thought about their system. Dallas wanted to win and was looking for innovative ways to accomplish that. Moving up in a particular round. Moving down in a particular round. Fake like you're supposed to trade. The Cowboys were about keeping teams guessing their intentions in the NFL draft. It just made the most sense. For the moves of the Cowboys, one thing never changed: finding talent. It's the only way to win. Talent. You can have good coaching, which is an added plus, but ultimately talent wins. Always has.

Before the draft unfolded, Dallas and the then-Washington Redskins were tied for the No. 3 overall pick in the draft based on their current record. So the NFL broke the tie the old-fashioned way: a coin flip. Washington won the flip and would pick No. 3. So Washington took Charley Taylor, the wide receiver from Arizona State.

Then it was time for Dallas.

There were several players the Cowboys thought about taking with their first-round pick. Defensive tackle Scott Appleton from Texas, Southern Cal quarterback Pete Beathard, wide receiver Paul Warfield from Ohio State, and defensive back Mel Renfro from Oregon were the top players of note.

Many across the league believed the Cowboys were taking Renfro with the fourth overall pick. Brandt had befriended Renfro during the draft process when the two were stuck at an airport in Eugene, Oregon. Brandt had also told Warfield the Cowboys were going to select him.

NFL teams were in a bidding war with the American Football League. Any player the AFL was looking at for its draft, so was the NFL. You needed scouts to stay in the homes of the players sometimes. That way when teams drafted them, a contract was on the living room table ready to be signed. It was almost like college recruiting when one school is chasing after a blue-chip prospect.

In terms of rebuilding the franchise, the Cowboys wanted an elite wide receiver, and this was Warfield. Landry had tremendous power in the Cowboys organization. For Brandt it was something he accepted because he was able to get the franchise to believe in some—if not most—of the players that he wanted. He knew the risks and understood not every player becomes what you want him to be. Landry informed Brandt the Cowboys were not taking Warfield. It was a disappointment for Brandt, but he moved forward thinking Renfro was the selection.

Renfro, however, had issues. He was a talented running back at the University of Oregon. He led the team in rushing for three straight seasons. But everything changed for Renfro the day president John F. Kennedy was assassinated. Upset that a man he believed in was taken away from the country, Renfro smashed a glass medicine cabinet. Renfro suffered ligament and tendon damage to the hand. Renfro went from being a legitimate first-round pick to there being questions if he could even play in the NFL. Well, of course, he could play, but an injury occurring just weeks before the NFL draft placed his expected high ranking on shaky ground.

The Cowboys held up the draft for Renfro. Schramm made a phone call to a doctor in Oregon and wanted an examination. If the doctor could determine Renfro's career wouldn't be derailed, he was the pick. In Chicago the feeling among NFL teams was split. *The Cowboys should take Renfro. The Cowboys should take a quarterback. The Cowboys should take a defensive player.* It was going to take a while to get all the necessary information to confirm Renfro's health.

The Cowboys were on the clock.

Back in the old days of the NFL draft, teams took their time. Phone calls, smoke breaks, double-checking, triple-checking, making sure scouts were in place with prospective draft selections—anything necessary to delay making a selection was done. But ultimately you needed to pick someone.

The Cowboys waited.

Waited.

Waited.

Waited.

And waited some more.

The Cowboys had teams guessing they would take Renfro. They had teams thinking he was their guy. In secret the Cowboys had no intentions of taking Renfro. NFL teams fell for it.

Dallas selected Appleton with its first-round pick. Appleton was also a first-round pick from the Houston Oilers in the AFL. He was going to play in the AFL.

This was the part of the NFL draft Brandt loved. Thinking the Cowboys were picking another player when in truth it wasn't even close. Brandt loved gamesmanship almost as much as picking the right players. This gamesmanship between teams brought long anxious moments with league executives. It also meant long moments between draft picks. The first round of the NFL draft lasted eight hours and five minutes. It was the longest first round in the history of the league. It angered NFL commissioner Pete Rozelle. After the first round, he told teams they had 30 minutes between draft selections.

Everyone ignored it.

After Rozelle's directive the San Francisco 49ers took an hour to make its second-round pick, which was University of Miami (Florida) quarterback George Mira. Dallas was on the clock for the second round and took six hours before picking Renfro. Schramm said at the time they were waiting for the medical information on Renfro. It was important to know if he could be relied on. Landry projected Renfro as a free safety despite his wonderful abilities as a running back in college. "All draft picks in a sense are a gamble," Landry told the *Dallas Times Herald*. "And with him we thought we would be better off gambling on the injury healing."

The draft, which started in the morning hours in Chicago, was now under the cold night of this midwest city. Players who were waiting to get drafted still hadn't. Meanwhile the Cowboys season was still ongoing. Meanwhile the NFL draft was still ongoing.

During the course of the early morning hours, the Cowboys drafted five quarterbacks. On the current roster sat Meredith. The star. The QB1.

Eddie LeBaron was the veteran backup nearing retirement. He made his name with Washington early in his career before finishing his final four seasons in Dallas. LeBaron was the Cowboys' first starting quarterback in their inaugural year in 1960. LeBaron, a sprite-like 5'9" and 168 pounds, finished that first season 0-9-1 as a starter. Before there was Meredith, LeBaron was the star quarterback. He wasn't alone during that first year. Meredith was a 22-year-old rookie on that team along with halfback Don McIlhenny from SMU; wide receiver Jim Doran, who was named to the Pro Bowl that season; and defensive lineman Don Healy, who recovered three fumbles. LeBaron was the cagy veteran until Meredith was ready to take over.

And then with Meredith, the star quarterback, and LeBaron retired, the other quarterback on this roster for the 1963 season was Sonny Gibbs, a second-round pick from Texas Christian University. The Cowboys were down on him. So in reality the Cowboys didn't have a true backup for Meredith.

The five signal callers taken were not a threat to Meredith. Landry had other ideas for three of the quarterbacks. Perry Lee Dunn was selected from the University of Mississippi. Landry said he was going to play defense. Billy Lothridge from Georgia Tech was a kicker, who set the NCAA record for field goals made. So it was easy to see where Landry was going with Lothridge. Bill Van Burkleo from Tulsa was a wide receiver in Landry's mind. Jerry Rhome also from Tulsa—and a transfer from SMU—did have some potential as a backup quarterback in the pros.

The Cowboys had drafted two quarterbacks, Dunn and Lothridge, before getting to a Heisman Trophy winner. When the 10th round started, San Francisco selected tackle Fred Posler from Texas A&M Commerce (then known as East Texas State). Philadelphia was next and selected running back Tom Boris from Purdue.

Then came the Cowboys.

It was just before dawn when Roger Staubach was picked in the 10th round with the 129th selection overall. Two picks later the Los Angeles Rams snagged quarterback Ron Smith. The Cowboys picked 20 players in that draft, and Staubach was an afterthought in the newspaper accounts of the NFL draft in Dallas. The first-round pick wasn't expected to play in Dallas, and the second-round pick had a wrist injury that gave the franchise concerns. There were five quarterbacks taken by the Cowboys. None was considered a serious impactful player at least in the immediate future. "Staubach, of course, is strictly a gamble," Landry said, according to the *Dallas Times Herald*. "If he finishes at Annapolis, he'll serve four years in the Navy before he can consider any other career. But if he happens not to graduate, we would have the rights to a splendid pro quarterback prospect."

Brandt saw the vision of what Staubach could become. Meredith was a standard dropback passer with some mobility and toughness to withstand the punishment of a vicious game. Staubach was not a threat to anyone—at least for the next few years. There was no guarantee Staubach would even play in the NFL. "Staubach?" Schramm said. "You just have to say we're building for the future. He ought to be a fine rookie in 1994. Imagine having a rear admiral as a rookie."

Some endorsement.

Brandt believed it was a smoke screen. He said if Staubach could play, Landry would utilize him. He was stubborn but understood the need to find the best way to use players.

But Staubach was years away from playing.

After the draft unfolded, Meredith attended the weekly Cowboys Club Luncheon on December 3. The starting quarterback of the Cowboys sat with sponsors, season ticket holders, and anyone who could sneak in for the luncheon to hear jokes about the five quarterbacks being taken. Instead of sitting at the head table, Meredith sat with the sponsors and season ticket holders 48 hours after losing a football game to the Giants at the Cotton Bowl. And now on the Tuesday after that game, Meredith learned five quarterbacks were taken in the draft, including the

Heisman Trophy winner in Staubach. While he was the star of the team, he didn't act like it—at least during this luncheon. This was Meredith's world. He was QB1, but yet the team he played for took five quarterbacks.

In reality, Staubach had a year of college eligibility at Navy then four more years serving his country. So this was a five-year plan before he could even reach the NFL, and then who knows how long before Staubach would take over a team? And based on what Landry and Schramm said, that was a major if. It was a plan few—other than Brandt—saw with positive results.

Staubach became one of the best college players in the country while at Navy. In the 1962 season, Staubach came off the bench to lead Navy in a victory against Cornell. He never lost the starting job after that.

One of the biggest games of his career came with President Kennedy watching. Kennedy enjoyed going to the Army–Navy game. The famed Army–Navy game was everything in college football. Navy was the underdog in this contest, but it upset Army 34–14. Staubach picked up four touchdowns—two passing and two rushing. "We had a very good connection," Staubach told *The Washington Post*. "We met him when he would go up to Nantucket. We used to train at Quonset Point, and he would come up in the helicopter and he was a Navy guy. PT 109. So I think he liked us better than Army, but he couldn't say that. He switched sides."

Staubach entered the 1963 season with modest expectations when in reality maybe they should have been higher. Staubach was nearly unstoppable. He was a scrambler with limited passing ability. He completed 66.7 percent of his passes with seven touchdowns and seven interceptions. He rushed for nine touchdowns.

Roger Staubach, who slings the ball early in his career, was the ultimate value pick, going from the 10th round to six-time Pro Bowler.

Staubach led Navy to a 9–2 finish and a No. 2 ranking in the Associated Press poll. If there was ever a college player that took over the sport, it was Staubach.

Navy's sports information director Budd Thalman sought something bigger for his starting quarterback. Thalman wanted to get Staubach into the Heisman Trophy race. The only way this was possible was by train. Thalman caught a train from Annapolis to Baltimore then to New York. The train ride took Thalman into Manhattan so he could meet with the college football writers over lunch and talk about his star quarterback. Thalman had index cards of Staubach's statistics. If the college football writers, the men deciding who was going to become the next Heisman Trophy winner, didn't know who Staubach was initially, Thalman made sure they knew.

What also helped Staubach was getting on the cover of *Time* magazine's October issue. He was also scheduled for the cover of *Life* magazine's late November issue. Staubach, who always took a humble approach to the attention he was getting, was excited about the *Life* magazine cover. The cover of the magazine had a picture of Staubach moving toward his left, looking downfield. Staubach, a right-handed throwing quarterback, would need to throw off-balance or most likely run the ball. It seemed like the perfect photo for Staubach, who commanded the attention of defenses with his abilities to throw and pass. The caption on Staubach's photo said everything: "The Greatest College Quarterback."

The cover had four headlines on the left of the front page of the magazine with a green background: "Negro Demands: Are they realistic?" "Army watch out! Here he comes. The Houdini of the backfield." "Wanamaker revolt against Deb Parties." "1913 Age of Innovation."

The assassination of President Kennedy changed everything. The cover of Staubach was scratched with more attention devoted to the death of the president. There were at least 300,000 copies made of the Staubach cover that were recalled to the *Life* offices. Staubach had a few copies. But it meant nothing now. A moving portrait of President Kennedy was on the cover instead. "My mother heard I was going to be on the cover of *Life* that week," Staubach said. "They destroyed most of them and brought them back and redid the whole cover. I was getting ready to go to class, a thermal dynamics class, and when I got to class I found out he was killed."

The world was shaken by the death of the president. It was hard for many to move on, especially Renfro, whose frustration with the death of the president was exhibited by the punch. It wasn't about football. It was life and what losing the president meant.

But the world moved on as difficult as it was. The Army–Navy game was coming up that winter. "The game was supposed to be a week from that Saturday," Staubach told NFL Films. "But it was delayed another week. It was just a lot of circumstances that are related to that football game and the president's death."

President Kennedy was killed November 22, 1963. Staubach received the Heisman Trophy four days later. When the college season ended, the biggest award for Staubach was in front of him. When the final tabulations of the Heisman Trophy vote were read, Staubach won in a landslide. He picked up 517 first-place votes. He totaled 1,860 votes. His nearest competitor was Georgia Tech's Lothridge with 65 first-place votes and 504 votes total. Sherman Lewis from Michigan State had 369 total votes with just 53 first-place selections. The player the Cowboys would eventually draft in the first round, Appleton, was fifth in the voting.

Staubach was not only the best player in college football, but also he won the Heisman Trophy due to his abilities on the field. He was a fantastic player with a bright future that caused problems for defenses that failed to contain him in the pocket. When the pocket collapsed, Staubach worked his magic, using his quickness and toughness to get down field.

Despite the success on the field and the award he received in addition to the Heisman Trophy, the loss of President Kennedy bothered him. It was hard for Staubach to enjoy the Heisman Trophy award. The night he received the award, the Army–Navy game got a new date: December 7. The game felt like 100 years away. It was difficult to prepare for the game, especially for Staubach who developed a fondness for President Kennedy. "The family asked the game to be played on his behalf," Staubach said. "So it was a special game."

Navy 21, Army 15.

Brandt meanwhile was visiting the Naval Academy looking for players and, of course, was doing homework on Staubach. Steve Belichick, an assistant coach at Navy, told Brandt about Staubach and his passing ability. Steve's son, Bill, who would later become one of the NFL's greatest coaches, formed a bond with Staubach. "I used to throw the football to him," Staubach remembered in a radio interview years later on KRLD-FM in Dallas. "His dad was there for 33 years."

Belichick mentioned in a 2017 interview with *N Magazine*, a publication based in Nantucket, admiring many people growing up while on the Navy base. Staubach was mentioned without any prodding. "When I look back on it, one of the things I learned at Annapolis, when I grew up around the Navy football teams in the early '60s—Joe Bellino, Roger Staubach, Coach Wayne Hardin, and some of the great teams they had—didn't know any differently," he said in the story. "I just assumed that's what football was. Guys were very disciplined. They worked very hard. They did extra things. They were always on time, alert, ready to go, team-oriented, unselfish. I thought that's the way it all was. I wasn't aware of it at the time, but I can see how that molded me."

Brandt kept an open mind about Staubach, knowing Meredith wasn't going anywhere at quarterback but also respected Steve Belichick's views on Staubach.

Having patience is something NFL teams needed in the 1960s. Sure team owners wanted quick results even back then, but patience and the foresight to see if a player could become a star needed time.

A quarterback was given time to succeed in the NFL.

In Staubach's final year, he struggled. He completed just 58.3 percent of his passes with four touchdowns and 10 interceptions. Health was an issue as Staubach injured his left heel in the season-opening victory against Penn State. He missed four games that year, and Navy's season went south with it. When the year was over, Navy was 3–6–1, a far cry from what it did the previous season.

With that season over, Staubach turned his life toward the military. Staubach always joked about being color blind, something that was determined when he enrolled into the Naval Academy. He failed to distinguish the port and starboard colors, which are red and green. With his years of playing football over now, Staubach turned to his service. He was assigned to the supply corps as a supply officer in Vietnam.

The United States was involved in an unpopular war in Vietnam. It didn't matter the viewpoint on the war from a political standpoint; many had conflicting thoughts on why the United States was there. In short, the Vietnam War was a conflict between the communist government of North Vietnam against South Vietnam. The United States, obviously, defended South Vietnam. Staubach arrived in Da Nang, South Vietnam, in 1966. He also was stationed at Chu Lia Naval Base. He was a lieutenant in the Navy in charge of 41 men handling ammunition supplies for Marines. "I wanted to do something to give back," Staubach said in a speech to fellow military veterans. "I wasn't on the battlefields. But I was out supporting. I was supporting the Naval support group out in the Nang. We had responsibilities."

Athletes serving in the military isn't something new. Baseball players Ted Williams, Al Bumbry, Bob Feller, and Jerry Coleman are some of the names to serve their country during wartime. Pittsburgh Steelers running back Rocky Bleier served in Vietnam, getting drafted after his rookie season in the NFL. Bleier lost part of his foot during an ambush. Bob Kalsu of the Buffalo Bills was the only active NFL player killed in the Vietnam War.

Staubach knew the history of athletes serving their country and took it seriously. He believed in supporting the country. He wasn't trying to make political statements, just wanting to fulfill his obligations with honor and dignity. "We were asked to do it," Staubach said of his service. "It wasn't a popular war."

Brandt kept close contact with Staubach after he was drafted. "We would send him balls," Brandt said. "He wanted to keep in shape, so I would send over a case of footballs to them. He would throw them around with the other troops. Then one day, he reached out saying the balls got lost."

The footballs were in a storage unit that blew up.

Brandt, always thinking ahead, sent more footballs to Staubach despite the extra cost.

The quarterback, the best in college football, was serving his country in Vietnam as part of a war where nearly 60,000 Americans would die. He wasn't just waiting for his time to end; he wanted to help in the only way possible.

Staubach had a roommate and former teammate on the football team, Tommy Holden, who was killed in Vietnam. The war was real to Staubach. It wasn't something that was far away for him. It impacted him immensely. "There's a camaraderie that's stayed with us," Staubach said in a 2018 story in *The Washington Post*. "Some of the guys I see quite a bit, we've also had a few tough situations. I was in Vietnam when our guard Tommy Holden was shot—we lost a few guys in Vietnam. So we have a history of staying together and bonding together."

As Staubach was serving his country, back in the states, the business of the NFL was moving on. The Cowboys finished the 1963 season at 4–10. One of the more ugly satisfying victories of the season occurred in the regular-season finale. Down by 10 points, Meredith rallied the Cowboys to a 28–24 victory against the St. Louis Cardinals. Despite getting sacked five times, Meredith threw two fourth-quarter touchdowns in the victory.

In 1964 Dallas improved to a 5–8–1 mark. Running back Don Perkins rushed for 768 yards and six touchdowns, and Meredith was picked off 16 times while throwing nine touchdowns in 12 games.

The Cowboys felt the 1965 season was a next step. NFL teams need hope. The program put in place had to see progress, and the Cowboys' plan set forth by Landry, Brandt, and Schramm was moving forward. Despite all the draft picks, draft trades, and potential deals falling through, at some point victories must occur.

The 1965 season started with so much hope. A 31–2 season-opening victory against the Giants followed by a 27–7 trashing of Washington gave the Cowboys a 2–0 start. The defense forced nine turnovers in the first two weeks of the season. Meredith was sacked seven times the first two weeks of the season but led an effective offense to help the Cowboys gain the confidence needed. But the Cowboys went on a five-game losing streak, and hope seemed lost. The label of an expansion franchise still loomed over the Cowboys.

This was a franchise not ready to take the next step. Maybe Landry wasn't the man for the job. He was a brilliant defensive coordinator with the Giants before leaving to take the Cowboys job. He wasn't in jeopardy of losing the Cowboys job, but the patience NFL teams need to have was becoming mandatory.

Dallas won five of its last seven games to finish the 1965 season at 7–7. It was the first .500 finish in franchise history. Progress. How much progress would be determined in the next season, which created the expectations to which Meredith eventually succumbed.

In 1966 the Cowboys finished 10–3–1. They had a 4–0 start to the season and then, despite some struggles, a four-game win streak from mid-November to early December. The regular season ended with a 17–7 victory against the Giants at Yankee Stadium.

The Cowboys had arrived.

Championship windows in the NFL are small. Coaches and team executives can say something different, but the truth is winning a title is hard. One season you're near the top of the league, and the next everything falls apart. Dallas wasn't trying to fall apart, especially with Meredith as its star quarterback. The Cowboys were the winners of the Eastern Division and scheduled to face the Packers, winners of the Western Division, in the NFL Championship Game. The winner would face the American Football League champion in the first Super Bowl. Imagine the Cowboys, a franchise that was built from scratch, playing in the first Super Bowl.

They were a seven-point underdog playing in their home stadium, the Cotton Bowl.

A close game had Meredith lead his team on a late fourth-quarter drive with Dallas trailing 34–27. Dallas faced a fourth and goal from the Green Bay 1. Meredith was under pressure from linebacker Dave Robinson as he rolled to his right. A missed block forced Meredith to throw with Robinson in his face. The pass was intended for speedy receiver Bob Hayes in the back of the end zone. Defensive back Tom Brown picked off the pass, ending the threat.

It was a heartbreaking loss—but not one that was going to damage the franchise. This was the breakthrough the Cowboys sought. Dallas had arrived on the scene.

So while Staubach was serving a year in Vietnam, which eventually moved into continued service in Annapolis, the Cowboys were moving forward with their franchise. In 1967 with Staubach still two years away from playing in the NFL, Meredith led the Cowboys back to the NFL Championship Game. The right to play in Super Bowl II was at stake again. This time the game was played in Green Bay. It was held on December 31, 1967. It was played in what was then the coldest game in franchise history: -15 degrees with a wind chill of-23. The grass field was slick with thin layer of ice, and traction was hard to find. This game was given the name of the Ice Bowl.

Dallas led 17–14 late in the fourth quarter. The roles were reversed in this championship game. Green Bay desired a late touchdown, and it was up to the Dallas defense to save the season. It was now the Cowboys' time to confirm their elite status. Green Bay quarterback Bart Starr dove in from the one-foot line for the game winner. Green Bay 21, Dallas 17.

It still didn't break the Cowboys resolve. It just wasn't their year. This was the Packers, a legendary franchise with a legendary coach and star players who were headed to the Hall of Fame.

But 1968 broke the Cowboys. They finished 12–2 and led the NFL in scoring with a 30.8 points per game average. There were 10 games where Dallas scored 25 or more points. This was the year.

It ended up shocking them.

Instead of the NFL Championship Game, the league expanded the playoffs, and this time the Cowboys were participating in the Eastern Conference Championship Game. So Dallas would not face Green Bay. It would face the Cleveland Browns. Meredith threw three interceptions and was benched. The turnovers led to 17 points, including a pick-six.

Dallas lost 31–20. "The most disappointing game I've ever played in my life," Meredith told NFL Films. "I could never get over that loss. I will never forget it. I think we just blew what was a tremendous opportunity for our team and I think I blew it more than anybody else there."

This emotion from Meredith was hard to bypass. Title windows are small. You never know what happens the next season because so many different things can happen. Meredith had enough. Meredith announced his retirement from the NFL.

It was a stunning announcement from a player considered in his prime. He was 30, a three-time Pro Bowler, who had been named the 1966 NFL Player of the Year. He led the Cowboys to eight game-winning drives. He was a second-team All-Pro in the 1966 and 1968 seasons. He was a star player who was popular with fans but took heavy criticism in the media for how the seasons ended. Meredith was a leader in the locker room with an infectious personality. "While Meredith is always thought of as that smiling, cheerful personality, fact of the matter is that he was one of the toughest players we ever had," Brandt wrote for NFL.com. "Despite the skinny legs and the fact he never really lifted weights, he was one of the toughest guys you'll ever come across."

Then he was gone along with that window the Cowboys were fighting to get through. For years the expansion franchise turned into a title contender that didn't win the big one. It lost to Green Bay in consecutive seasons with a right to play in the Super Bowl, losing in the famed Ice Bowl. It overcame being a home team underdog—only to lose on a Meredith interception. And then in the final year of their window, the first star of this team was benched. It was just too much for Meredith to accept. He left on his terms, knowing he could still play in the NFL. The health issues he fought through and the criticism thrown his way were just too much at that stage of his life.

The Cowboys were trying to move on without him. They needed someone to help. Craig Morton was the Cowboys' 1965 first-round pick drafted fifth overall. Morton was next up to push the Cowboys to another title window that was getting smaller by the year. Meredith would no longer lead them here. It was Morton's time.

You could look back at that 1964 Cowboys draft class for the next quarterback. Staubach finished his college football career, having won the Heisman Trophy, Maxwell Award, and Walter Camp Award. He broke 28 records at Navy and led them to a high ranking in the 1963 season. Staubach still remembers the two losses: on a Friday night in Dallas to SMU and in the Cotton Bowl that season. Football remained in his future, but more important things were forthcoming. "My heroes are those that made a career of their military responsibilities," he said in an interview with the Navy alumni.

Staubach enlisted in the military by accident in some ways. While a senior co-captain on the football team at Purcell High School in Cincinnati, Navy coach Hardin came to recruit Staubach's center. While Hardin was watching videotape of the center, he noticed Staubach and went after him, too. Staubach had made an oral commitment to Purdue, but after talking with Hardin and family, he elected to go to the military. At first, he was supposed to attend a preparatory school, but Staubach didn't want that. So he elected to enroll at New Mexico Military Institute in Roswell, New Mexico.

Staubach would say the year he spent in New Mexico helped him prepare for life in Annapolis. He would eventually graduate from the Naval Academy in June 1965. He spent a year in Vietnam before getting stationed in Naval Air Station in Pensacola, Florida. His military service ended in 1968.

Meanwhile, the Cowboys were a franchise trying to replace Meredith. It was difficult. The reality for Staubach taking over at the age of 27 was still remote. It didn't seem real. Almost five years after getting drafted and throwing footballs to servicemen and ex-players, Staubach's dream of playing in the NFL was becoming real.

Or was it?

Morton was the established starter for a franchise that was close to a title. The biggest challenge for Staubach was his passing ability. In college his legs allowed him to get away from pressure. The NFL was a different game. The players were faster, stronger, and smarter. Pro coaches spent long hours devising schemes to beat teams. College wasn't that way, at least for the coaches.

Staubach had to make the adjustment. The long-term vision for Staubach was coming into focus. Brandt saw the movement in Staubach while he was the quarterback at Navy. He just needed Landry to see it, too.

Landry's focus was on the veteran quarterbacks. He suddenly lost Meredith, a man with experience who couldn't win a big game when it mattered. It wasn't totally Meredith's fault, but the ending of his career didn't help. A benching in his final game. A dejected look in front of reporters after that loss to Cleveland to end the 1968 season.

Staubach was in Florida getting ready to finish his service and preparing for an unknown future in the NFL. Meredith was 30 when he retired. Morton, the man who took over, was 26, and here came Staubach, a 27-year-old rookie who hadn't played competitive football in years, as the new backup.

The Cowboys were a franchise ascending—but to what few would know. Staubach was trying to fit in with Morton and not make mistakes. He went from needing a well-deserved campaign to win the Heisman Trophy at Navy, becoming a pick of the future for the Cowboys, serving his country in a war his own country didn't like to possibly starting at quarterback in the NFL.

The kid with the crewcut, an only child born and raised in Cincinnati who signed up for the military thanks to his high school center, was finding that focus in his life now. Landry was bringing him back to reality. It was perfect. It was what Staubach needed. "His running ability when he first came into the league was really a cover-up from lack of experience," Landry said of Staubach. "There's no way a quarterback until he learns to read defenses, until he learns to move the defense around, [can] do the things he wants to do from the pocket. Until he learns that, then he's going to rely on what his best quality is, and Roger's greatest quality when he first started was running."

The wait was worth it for Staubach and the Cowboys. While Staubach had to battle Morton for the starting job, he eventually took over the job. He led the Cowboys to a pair of Super Bowl titles. When his 11-year career ended, Staubach was named to six Pro Bowls, led the NFL in touchdown passes with 23 in 1973, and led the Cowboys to 21 game-winning drives and 13 comeback victories. One of the greatest comebacks in league history came in the 1975 NFC Divisional Round when Captain Comeback threw a Hail Mary pass to wide receiver Drew Pearson to defeat the Minnesota Vikings. Staubach's career ended due to the number of concussions he endured at a time when the NFL reviewed the head injury with minimal attention. The Pro Football Hall of Famer reached unparalleled success with the Cowboys. Staubach is revered in Cowboys history as one of the greats against whom all other quarterbacks are measured.

2

ED "TOO TALL" JONES

BEING THE NO. 1 overall pick of the NFL draft comes with tremendous pressure. The expectations arrive from the team, player, fanbase, and media. Not every player can handle the pressures or understand the magnitude of it. If a team has that No. 1 overall selection, it's because the previous season was poorly constructed.

In the case of the 1974 NFL Draft, the Dallas Cowboys obtained the No. 1 pick because of the Houston Oilers' own mistakes. It was mismanagement of what the NFL was turning into that gave the Cowboys the No. 1 pick. In the early 1970s, NFL teams used veteran players to move up the standings more so than building through the draft.

The Miami Dolphins won back-to-back Super Bowls (VII and VIII) with veteran players in their early 30s. The 1972, 17–0 title team was led by 38-year-old quarterback Earl Morrall.

Miami defeated a veteran Washington Redskins team in Super Bowl VII. Washington had several players over 30, including quarterback Billy Kilmer, wide receiver Charley Taylor, and linebackers Jack Pardee and Chris Hanburger. Some of the Dolphins' best players were 30 years or older with some notables in wide receiver Paul Warfield, tight end Marv Fleming, and middle linebacker Nick Buoniconti. So having vets, players who understood how to win after years of getting beaten up by losses and heartbreak in previous playoff games, appeared the right move.

The draft, as valuable as it may have been, sometimes seemed like a novel concept.

Patience was a valuable tool when it came to some NFL teams. Waiting on draft picks to not only make the rosters, but also become reliable contributors once they got on the field was essential to success. While some teams utilized veterans, particularly those who were homegrown talent, others waited for the limited availability of free agency or trades to make moves.

Dallas was not one of those teams.

As an expansion team, the Cowboys used the draft to grow into a title contender. They had no choice. Sure, there were veteran players on the Cowboys, who signed as free agents, but the core of the teams in the late 1960s and early 1970s was from the NFL draft. In the 1971 season, Dallas had just won the franchise's first Super Bowl. The Cowboys finally arrived on the scene as an elite team. There were flaws; most teams have something needing improvement, but the Cowboys of the 1970s had homegrown talent. Building in the draft was still in their blood because it was clear in the results. Of the eight Pro Bowlers in the 1971 Super Bowl title season, five were draft picks, including two first-round picks in Bob Lilly and John Niland.

Yet, some NFL teams believed in something else.

The Oilers had just finished the 1972 season, having missed the postseason for a third consecutive year. The Oilers offense averaged just 11.7 points per game while allowing 27.1 points per game on defense. The Oilers committed 12 turnovers the last three games and finished the season with a 61–17 loss to the Cincinnati Bengals. That spring the Oilers decided to change their approach by taking the advice of general manager Sid Gillman. He contacted Cowboys executive Gil Brandt and proposed a trade. The Oilers wanted veterans because why not? That was how the NFL was moving. Draft picks took too long to develop.

Established stars were the optimal way to progress in the NFL. A look at Washington and Miami with their veteran players was a testament to this. Washington's coach George Allen retooled the football team using veteran players in their 30s. Fans nicknamed the team "The Over the Hill Gang." That Washington team led by Allen's passionate speeches relied on veterans and reached the Super Bowl.

This was the formula Gillman wanted to follow. Brandt understood where Gillman was coming from, but his value was on the draft more so than trading for veteran players. So Houston traded first- and third-round picks to Dallas for defensive end Tody Smith and wide receiver Billy Parks.

Tody Smith was the younger brother of Baltimore Colts defensive lineman Bubba Smith. Bubba Smith had more of a name than Tody, and it seemed if you're giving up a first-round pick, maybe Bubba Smith was a better selection. Tody Smith was a first-round pick by the Cowboys in 1971, the 25th pick overall. In two seasons Smith had five sacks, spanning 17 games. He played in seven games for the Super Bowl-winning Cowboys in 1971.

Parks was a sixth-round selection by the San Diego Chargers, and his rookie season was his most productive. He caught 41 passes for 609 yards with four touchdowns. But he was traded to the Cowboys for troubled running back Duane Thomas, along with fellow halfback Mike Montgomery. Thomas failed to report to the Chargers and was eventually placed on the reserve list, making him ineligible for the season. Parks had caught 18 passes for just 298 yards and one touchdown in 1972. Parks was a backup receiver—not someone you believed could help an offense long term in the passing game.

The trade was a steal for the Cowboys, considering the two backup players they gave up for the draft capital. So the Cowboys entered the 1974 draft with two first-round picks. The only question was how high the Cowboys would draft with the Oilers' selection.

Houston's 1973 season was a disaster. Gillman took over for Bill Peterson after a 0–5 start. In one of their worst losses of the season, the Oilers committed nine turnovers and just five first downs in a 33–7 loss to the Pittsburgh Steelers. When the season ended, the Oilers finished 1–13. Houston committed a turnover in every game it played in the 1973 season, averaging 14.2 points and allowing 31.9 points per game.

Gillman was given the job full time by owner Bud Adams because of his belief he would push this franchise to greater heights. Gillman was one of the great minds in football. He was well-respected for his gameplans and his mentorship of younger coaches. One of the main reasons why the NFL and the AFL decided to play its champions against each other was due to Gillman's suggestions to NFL commissioner Pete Rozelle.

While Gillman was trying to fix the Oilers, the Cowboys' 1973 season ended with them winning the tiebreaker over Washington to clinch first place in the NFC East. Dallas finished 10–4 with the second best offense in the NFL. Quarterback Roger Staubach was tied for first with 23 touchdown passes, and running back Calvin Hill finished third with 1,142 rushing yards. Two years removed from a Super Bowl title, the Cowboys defeated the Los Angeles Rams in the NFC Divisional Playoffs but lost to the Minnesota Vikings 27–10 in the NFC title game. With their season now over, the Cowboys entered the draft in excellent shape. Dallas had the No. 1 overall pick—thanks to the poor year by Houston—and its original pick at No. 22 overall.

Offense wasn't a problem for the Cowboys. Finding upgrades on defense was key. Linebacker Chuck Howley had retired after playing in just one game of the 1973 season at the age of 37. Howley suffered a knee injury in a regular-season game against Washington the previous season. Howley announced his retirement—only to return, but after playing in just one game, it was determined he couldn't play anymore.

There was 34-year-old defensive tackle Bob Lilly, and he just finished his 13ᵗʰ NFL season. Lilly was the first player drafted by the Cowboys. He played through the lean years of the franchise and was rewarded with a Super Bowl title. Lilly had never missed a game during his career and wasn't preparing to do so then. Yet, he was getting older.

Middle linebacker Lee Roy Jordan was 32 when the 1973 season ended and he was coming off a Pro Bowl berth after picking off a career-high six interceptions. Jordan was considered a solid player, but there were questions about for how much longer given his age.

As far as the two key defensive backs: cornerback Mel Renfro was 32, and safety Cornell Green was 33.

How long before you start to get younger?

In the 1973 draft, the Cowboys made six of their 17 selections defensive players. That was led by defensive end Harvey Martin, a talented player from East Texas State, in the third round. Also, linebacker Rodrigo Barnes was picked in the seventh round. The Cowboys defense allowed 14.5 points per game, which ranked seventh best in the NFL.

NFL teams sought younger talent as quickly as possible. The NFL game in the 1970s relied on veterans, but when an older player started to slip, head coaches and general managers started looking. Finding players wasn't the problem, especially with an NFL draft that would last for hours and go for 20 rounds. Finding talented players with so many selections was the issue.

The Cowboys went to great lengths to find players. It really had no choice when it was an expansion team. With the Cowboys as a title contender, the same formula of building in the draft and waiting on prospects—such was the case with Staubach drafted in 1964—was an important part of their success. Brandt knew this better than most. He didn't care where he needed to go. He would just take a look at a particular player. He would send scouts to various places across the country for talent. Brandt even asked Green to do it.

Green was the All-Pro safety who knew talent. It was an odd situation to be in if you were Green. Here was the talent looking for more talent—maybe even finding his replacement one day. But Green trusted the Cowboys, and the Cowboys trusted Green, so the partnership was welcomed. If anything, Green knew what he was doing. He also understood what coach Tom Landry was looking for when it came to defensive players. Yes, the Cowboys had the formula for acquiring talent in the draft.

One area where the Cowboys weren't afraid to draft from was the bountiful talent from Historically Black Colleges and Universities. NFL teams didn't have a huge roster with Black players. Some teams had quotas, or their owners refused any Black players. With integration more and more Black football players were getting chances to compete at traditional White colleges and universities. It didn't curtail Black players from still going to HBCUs. The first player drafted from a HBCU was tackle Jack Spinks from Alcorn State in the 11th round (126th overall) by the Steelers. While there were Black players in the NFL, few were from HBCUs, where some NFL teams didn't believe the talent was to the level of the predominantly White institutions. But there was talent in HBCUs if you were willing to find it.

Over the years the Cowboys looked to the rosters of HBCUs to find talent. The Cowboys made their first draft selection from an HBCU in 1962 when they drafted wide receiver Donnie Davis from Southern University. In 1964 Bob Hayes, the speedy Olympian, was selected in the seventh round from Florida A&M. In 1966 the Cowboys drafted two players from HBCUs: wide receiver Arthur Robinson, a seventh-round pick from Florida A&M, and half-back Lewis Turner, a 14th-round pick from Norfolk State. Both players never played for the Cowboys, but the franchise proved it wasn't shy about going to the Deep South to find players. One of its best players was found at an HBCU in Rayfield Wright, an offensive tackle from Fort Valley State in the 1967 draft. Wright was a seventh-round selection and earned his third consecutive All-Pro berth following the 1973 season.

What was also fueling the influx of Black players in the NFL was the AFL. The upstart league drafted Black players, especially from HBCUs. Buck Buchanan—from the HBCU Grambling State—was the first overall player taken in the 1963 AFL Draft. The NFL's New York Giants selected Buchanan in the 19th round. The increase of salaries was also a major factor for some prospective draft picks when it came down to NFL and AFL teams. If a player could receive more from the AFL team, then he bypassed the NFL's offer. Some players negotiated between the leagues, hoping for more money from the NFL, the league they really wanted to participate in. The AFL was the spark professional football was seeking, whether the NFL liked it or not. Several of its owners like Al Davis from the Oakland Raiders and Adams in Houston, among others, pushed the boundaries of what the NFL was.

The NFL was the established league. Conservative. The AFL was the rebel without a pause.

In some ways the NFL wasn't ready for what the AFL represented: change. NFL teams' ability to find players was changing, too, and HBCUs played a factor in that. So it wasn't a surprise when Green was sent to Nashville, Tennessee, to check on the talent of Tennessee State.

John Merritt was a cigar-chomping legend in the city of Nashville. Merritt earned his status by coaching Tennessee State, a HBCU. Merritt coached at Jackson State from 1953 to 1962 before leaving for what was then Tennessee A&I. Merritt stalked the sidelines, demanding his players play a physical brand of football, particularly on defense. Merritt introduced a pro-style offense to the college game by offering multiple sets that encouraged a wide-open game with more passing than what the college game was used to seeing. Not only was the style of play unique, Merritt and his coaching staff wore these long jackets that said: "Tennessee State Football Staff." It was a distinct feel to Tennessee State. You knew it was a big-time school regardless of its status as a HBCU.

In Merritt's first season at Tennessee State, he went 6–3. But in the 1960s, Merritt's teams won two Black College National Championships in 1965 and 1966. In 1967 defensive end Claude Humphrey was named an All-American by *Time* magazine. It was the first time a player from Tennessee A&I, now Tennessee State, was named to an All-American team. The first seven seasons of Merritt's career (1963–69) at Tennessee State became a scout's dream. Merritt produced many players from his teams that were drafted from the NFL, including two first-rounders: wide receiver Eldridge Dickey and Jim Marsalis. Dan Pride and Fletcher Smith were drafted by only the AFL in 1966, and Robert Reed was drafted by both the NFL and AFL in 1965. By going to Tennessee State, you were not only playing for a coach establishing himself as one of the best in the country, but NFL and AFL teams also were going to find you.

Merritt was seeking talent. The Jones family, meanwhile, was under siege in Jackson, Tennessee.

Ed Jones was a basketball and baseball player at East Side High School. But he wanted to play football. Jones was this fantastic baseball and basketball player, and there was a growing sentiment in the community of Jackson that playing baseball and basketball was in his future. But Jones' brother-in-law, James Matthews, wanted something different. He could tell Jones' long frame—6'5" in high school—could provide an offense with a talented tight end or wide receiver. Matthews was a pretty good athlete himself growing up in Jackson. He injured his knee, ending any possible college stardom. But James knew talent. He saw it in Ed Jones.

There was an issue, though. The community wouldn't stand for it.

East Side High School didn't have a football program so if Ed Jones was going to play that sport he needed to transfer. "To be eligible I had to live with my sister and brother-in-law," Ed Jones said. "I had to grow up on a farm in the country. I couldn't just drive in or what have you and play at Merry High School."

Merry High School had football. So Ed Jones moved from the heart of Jackson to the outskirts, the country, to live with his sister, Parlie, and her husband, James Matthews. It didn't sit well with people who didn't approve of a talented athlete like Ed Jones transferring from one school to another for athletic reasons. And to play football. His future was in basketball. But sometimes a person has to find his or her own path, and that's where Ed Jones took a stand for himself and his family. "My own town turned against me when I tried out for football," Ed Jones said. "They thought they would finally have a person representing Jackson, Tennessee, in baseball or basketball...I was a very good baseball and basketball player, an All-American in both."

Imagine Jones, who had scholarship offers from almost every school in the country, posting up in the paint in basketball or batting with that enlarged strike zone. Colleges wanted that athletic ability and the smarts that came with it. "And so [the community] kind of turned against me, and my family got involved," Jones said. "[Matthews] felt responsible for that. People were saying, 'What are you doing letting this man play football? He's a great basketball and baseball player.' We didn't have football in high school, and I transferred my senior year under the influence of my brother-in-law to see what it was like."

After enrolling at Merry High School, Jones was prepared for a football season at tight end. But his coaches had different feelings on the subject. "Well, my baseball and basketball coach was also the football coach," Jones said. "He let me practice, but he didn't play me. He didn't want me getting hurt because he wanted me for basketball and baseball. We went to the state in baseball and we went to the state in basketball, and that's what he wanted."

Jones' high school coaches taught Jones everything about football from the cadence to catching the ball, running routes, even getting in and out of the huddle. The vision for Jones was to play basketball because that was his best sport. Coaches didn't want him to get hurt playing football so they taught him how to fall down when he was getting tackled. So he was getting somewhat of an education to perform in the sport he liked, but he really didn't know the nuances of it. "I absolutely loved football from Day One, even though I didn't have a clue what I was doing," Jones said. "I was trying out for tight end. I had good speed, good hands, and I was tall at the time. I was only 6'5"."

So after one year of practicing football at the high school level, Jones was going to get a scholarship...in basketball. Jones was an excellent basketball player, and no school was going to take a chance on him playing football, especially after he never played it on the organized level. So Jones received a scholarship to play basketball at Tennessee State.

Tennessee State hired a new coach in Ed Martin for the 1968–69 season. Tennessee State finished its first season under Martin at 14–12. It improved dramatically the next season with a 21–8 mark, which included three three-game win streaks and a five-game win streak. Jones, wearing No. 52, wasn't having the impact in college that was occurring in high school. After two seasons in 1970 and 1971, Martin took Jones to meet Coach Merritt. Jones said Merritt looked at his length and said he needed to get him on the football field. Jones was still learning the sport and played tight end. Yet, Joe Gilliam Sr. was Jones' defensive coach and looked at the possibilities of how tremendous this young player could be on defense.

Jones' size—he grew from 6'5" in high school to nearly 6'8" in college—was a problem not only for opponents, but also for his school. For Jones' first football practice, the equipment manager couldn't find football pants that fit. Jones ventured out onto the practice fields with football pants that landed just above the knees. One of Jones' new teammates laughed upon seeing this while the two were having lunch. Jones recalled the new teammate saying he "was too tall to play football," and hence the nickname "Too Tall" became real.

Ed Jones, now Ed "Too Tall" Jones, made an impact at Tennessee State. It took some time, though.

At Tennessee State Jones was a scout-team tight end. He would give the first-team defense fits because of his size and ability to catch passes. Yet, Gilliam was worried. He told "Too Tall" he needed to fall "gracefully."

Jones took that to mean don't get hurt. "You don't know how you're going to fall and where you're going to land," he said. "Whatever you do, it's got to be graceful, or you're going to injure yourself."

In addition to learning the game, Jones was pushed to become tougher and he met the challenge. "They didn't want anybody out there unless you were serious," he said. "They tried to run me off. If I had one fight, I had 100. Once they realized they couldn't run me off, Coach Gilliam called me to the side one day."

"Looks like you're taking this game pretty seriously," Gilliam told Jones.

Jones gave one-word answers as he tried to figure out what his position coach was saying.

"If you are lucky enough to get through college and play at the next level you would be one of the tallest to play in the game," Gilliam said.

Okay.

"The average NFL career is four years."

All right.

"Most injuries occur in the fourth quarter when fatigue sets in," the coach continued.

Okay.

"You have to be one of the best conditioned athletes on the field to get to that level. If you're willing to do my program, I'm willing to work with you and I think you got it."

That was the talk Jones needed. But Jones added an extra layer to his conditioning. He went to the track team.

Not the men's track program.

Jones worked out with the Tennessee State women's track club. They were called the Tigerbells, a star-studded program that had gold medal-winning sprinters such as Wilma Rudolph, Wyomia Tyus, Madeline Manning, and Edith McGuire.

Jones' goal was to be in optimal shape for the fourth quarter of games. "Great track stars, those ladies went on to win gold medals in the Olympics," Jones said. "I would go work out with them. I was out there trying, but I had dirt in my face. I just made a promise to myself that if you get me, it won't be because of fatigue. I'm giving 110 percent."

In 1971 everything changed when several defensive players got hurt along the defensive line. Gilliam moved Jones to defensive end. It was supposed to be a short-term venture until some of the starters, including defensive end Will Wynn, returned from injury. But "Too Tall" Jones morphed into something Gilliam needed: another talented defensive end. "He wouldn't let me go back to offense," Jones said. "It was one of the best things that ever happened because I absolutely loved playing defense. I enjoyed offense, but I loved defense. Anytime you play in a contact sport with the number of injuries [we] had back then, there's no way I would have played tight end and never missed a game in college. It was all because [of] being in the best shape all the time."

Over time, "Too Tall" Jones became not only a dependable player for Tennessee State, but also someone who would take over. Jones picked up pass rush and run techniques while practicing at defensive end. He seemed more natural rushing the passer than running routes to catch passes. Jones also stayed with basketball. He lettered in both sports in college. "If I hadn't liked football, I was going to drop football and just play basketball and baseball. I made honorable mention All-American."

Jones did give up basketball after his sophomore season because of the greater potential in football. It was a remarkable transformation for Jones. He never played high school football, transferring in his senior year just to get on the field but was denied because he was too raw. Then he became a highly-decorated college football player. When that occurs, NFL teams come calling. NFL teams, especially the Cowboys, want talent regardless of where that particular individual was going to school.

Jones was named to All-American teams in the 1972 and 1973 seasons. He finished his career with 40 career sacks and produced one season with 12 sacks. During his time at Tennessee State, Jones played on teams that went 11–0, 9–1, and 11–1. Tennessee State was the Black national champion for the 1970 season when it went 11–0. In Jones' final season, 1973, Tennessee State went 10–0 while dominating its opponents the entire campaign. Merritt's defense shut out two opponents and allowed just 27 points the final five games of the season.

It was a talented defense that not only included Jones, but also linebacker Waymond Bryant. The talent from Tennessee State was tremendous with Jones leading the way. Wide receiver John Holland and tackle Greg Kindle were two other players who were part of a deep senior class. "It wasn't just me they were coming to look at," Jones said. "But it gave—regardless of who they were coming to look at, if they weren't coming to look at me initially—they had a chance to see me because we were winning, and I had a good [senior] year."

Jones didn't act like a star player. He wanted the tutelage of other players before him. His brother-in-law suggested he watch former Tennessee State end Humphrey in addition to Joe "Turkey" Jones, another defensive end.

In high school Ed Jones drove from Jackson to Nashville to watch Humphrey and Turkey Jones play. It was his first look at his future. He was a basketball player yearning for something else, and that was football. He loved basketball, too, also remembering some of the great basketball players that came from Tennessee State. Yet, if he was going to become a full-time football player, he had perfect examples for emulating. While he was being groomed to play tight end that senior year of high school, he made note of what the defensive line was doing. "I tried to pattern my game after [Humphrey] and Joe 'Turkey' Jones," Ed Jones said. "I admired Claude Humphrey in high school and I loved how Joe 'Turkey' Jones could run because I had good speed, too. I had some good guys I could pattern my game after."

Green, the player and scout, informed the Cowboys about Ed Jones. Brandt, the executive in charge of personnel, had good feelings about the reports on him. So the Cowboys sent scouts and coaches to Nashville to speak with Merritt about his players. One problem: Merritt wouldn't let scouts measure his players. He refused NFL teams' request to time his players in the 40-yard dash or perform individual drills. Merritt wasn't anti-NFL—how could he be considering the success his program was having in getting players to the pros—but he wanted NFL teams to grade his players based on their performances on the field. It also gave his program a bit of a mystery because an NFL team couldn't fit a particular player in a position based on workouts on practice fields.

If you wanted to know Jones' height, you had to ask him, but measuring him wasn't happening. Want to know how fast Holland was? Well, that was guesswork, too. "We didn't have any of that stuff," Jones said about workouts for NFL scouts. "Tennessee State didn't allow teams to time us or weigh us. We were probably the only college team that didn't allow that."

Tennessee State was similar in how the Cowboys operated during the draft. Merritt kept opponents guessing about how heavy or tall his players actually were. "I was so thin, 235 pounds," Jones said. "But I had the biggest shoulder pads and biggest thigh and knee pads. They listed me in the program at 270. What we were trying to do was intimidate other college teams."

Following his senior season, Jones discovered the Cowboys had the No. 1 overall pick of the NFL draft. Jones didn't believe a defensive lineman could go No. 1 overall. Jones only cared about getting drafted in the first round because he believed he did enough to warrant that. During the season former players from Tennessee State would return to Nashville and tell Jones he could play in the NFL. The men he looked up to like Humphrey and "Turkey" Jones were in the NFL. "Too Tall" Jones not only saw them play on Saturdays while he was in high school, but also read about their exploits as NFL players. Humphrey and Jones set the standard for defensive linemen from Tennessee State who reached the NFL.

Jones now believed it was possible. The Cowboys, thanks to the trade with the Oilers, were thinking they might have the No. 1 overall pick.

The Oilers were terrible after winning a combined two games in the 1972 and 1973 seasons, and their own rebuilding process skewed toward veterans, while the Cowboys wanted to get younger along the defensive line. So when the 1973 NFL and college football seasons ended, several college players entered the mix for the No. 1 pick.

The quarterback class was considered weak with the top quarterbacks being Arizona State's Danny White, Boston College's Gary Marangi, and Kansas' David Jaynes. Penn State running back John Cappelletti was the reigning Heisman Trophy winner. Cappelletti won the Heisman Trophy in 1973, but the Cowboys didn't need a running back. Dallas employed Hill, who was named to the Pro Bowl for the 1972 season after rushing for 1,036 yards with six touchdowns. The next season Hill rushed for 1,142 yards with another six touchdowns. Selecting Cappelletti didn't seem sound at this particular time.

Getting younger along the defensive line was paramount to the Cowboys. The first player selected by the Cowboys before their first season of play in 1960, Lilly was considered Mr. Cowboy. But one of the great defensive linemen in league history was getting older. He would be 35 at the start of the 1974 season after coming off his 10th consecutive Pro Bowl berth.

There, though, was youth along the defensive line. Jethro Pugh, who could play end and tackle, was going to be 30 by Week One of the '74 season. Larry Cole, the left defensive end, was still considered in his prime at 27. In the last two NFL drafts, 1972 and 1973, the Cowboys selected four defensive linemen. In 1972 they took Richard Amman in the 10th round from Florida State and Alphonso Cain in the 17th round from Bethune-Cookman. Both were picked but didn't make the roster, and neither did North Carolina A&T's Lonnie Leonard.

The next draft Martin was picked in the third round. A local player born and raised in Dallas, Martin attended South Oak Cliff and then played college in Commerce, Texas, nearly two hours away from Dallas. Martin, a defensive tackle, had an outstanding rookie year. He finished the season with nine sacks and had future written all over him. Now it was about finding a partner with him if Lilly was near retirement.

NFL teams are always divided between selecting the best player available and drafting for need. The 1974 draft had a weak quarterback class with one or maybe two running backs worth taking in the first round but none with the first overall pick. The defensive and offensive lines, however, were stocked with talented players.

Selecting the No. 1 overall pick is normally slated for quarterbacks, running backs, and dynamic defensive players. Offense not only carries the draft, but also the first overall pick. The first NFL draft took place in 1936, and it wasn't until linebacker Chuck Bednarik was drafted No. 1 overall by the Philadelphia Eagles in 1949 that a defensive player was picked No. 1 overall.

Defensive players were always valued players, but offensive players were sexy picks. Drafting a quarterback won the press conference and garnered the better headlines compared to an offensive and defensive lineman. As the draft progressed, defensive players were no longer forgotten members of draft classes. Things changed over time. Before the 1974 draft, two defensive players, John Matuszak, a defensive end in 1973, and Walt Patulski, another defensive end in 1972, were taken No. 1 overall. In fact, it had been three years since a quarterback was taken No. 1 overall. Jim Plunkett was the first pick of the draft by the New England Patriots in 1971.

The Cowboys had an opportunity to make it three consecutive years a defensive player was taken No. 1 overall. In Jones' junior season, Green was trying to tell him. Jones didn't want to believe him. What Green was saying didn't seem possible. *First overall pick?*

In the offseason Green left the shoulder pads at home and became a scout. He flew to Nashville and drove to Tennessee State's campus to check on the prospective draft picks. "He talked to the coaching staff, he talked to the teachers, the students," Jones said. "He just [was] getting a feel of what not only myself, but some other guys, they were looking at was like personality wise."

Green confided in Jones during one of these offseason talks. "Dallas is seriously considering drafting you if you're available," Green said.

The young player said he just listened. He heard stories about NFL teams telling prospective draft picks one thing, and something else happening. Of course, why would a player from Tennessee State, a Division II school, have the No. 1 pick of the draft?

Jones finished his senior season as one of the top players in the country, and numerous NFL teams wanted to fly him for visits to their facilities. The night before the NFL draft, on January 28, 1974, the Cowboys called Jones and informed him he was coming to Dallas. "I said, 'Okay, this is probably not that serious,'" Jones said.

Cowboys' officials told Jones he could bring two people with him. So Jones asked his college coach, Merritt, and his brother-in-law, Matthews, to come on the trip. The trio was staying at a hotel down the street from the Cowboys offices off Interstate 75. It was early evening when the Cowboys told the men to have dinner on the team. "The Cowboys told us to go to a restaurant of our choice," Jones said. "Bring the receipt back. They would reimburse us."

The three men decided to take advantage of a free meal, especially one from the Cowboys, and wanted to make sure it was of quality. "My brother-in-law and coach were big men, big eaters," Jones said. "I was underweight. Same thing for me. I was just trying to eat all I could to gain weight."

After asking people at the hotel, the trio elected to eat steak. There was a steakhouse nearby, and the men walked to it. It was at that dinner that Matthews and Merritt wanted to tell Jones what they thought of the NFL draft. Matthews and Merritt told Jones he wasn't going to be the first overall pick despite the Cowboys having him in for a visit. Jones visited with the New York Giants and the Chargers in the buildup of the draft. It made more sense for those teams to pick him over the Cowboys.

Jones was a talented a player with the credentials, size, and speed NFL teams were looking for, but he came from a Division II program. Players from Division II programs, especially teams from HBCUs, don't get picked No. 1 overall. "We need to tell you something," Matthews said over dinner. "You're not going to be the first player chosen tomorrow."

The two men had serious looks on their faces. It didn't matter what Green had told Jones the year before about the Cowboys plans. "Why are we here?" Jones asked.

The draft had running back Cappelletti and quarterbacks Jaynes, White, and Marangi, who were highly regarded. John Dutton, a defensive tackle from Nebraska, was also a top prospect. Jones was a top prospect, too, but being No. 1 didn't seem realistic to people close to him. "They convinced me," Jones said of not believing he would go No. 1.

So another decision was made: live it up. "Hey, man, let's order the best wine and the biggest steaks they have here tonight and have ourselves a good time," Matthews told the party.

Jones and Merritt agreed. "I wasn't a drinker, but I did order the biggest steak they had," Jones said. "We had a great time."

The 1974 NFL Draft was held in New York at the Americana Hotel in Manhattan. It was one of the few thousand hotel rooms in the city. Normally, Brandt would attend the draft fielding phone calls from Tex Schramm and Landry, who were in Dallas. Brandt worked the room of other NFL executives to foster a trade or fake out other teams into thinking the Cowboys were going to make a trade.

But with the No. 1 pick of the draft, Brandt was in Dallas. He wanted to be here for the Cowboys' first attempt at the No. 1 overall selection in franchise history. He got up early and made sure everyone was on the same page with the draft pick. Landry was good. Schramm was good. The other scouts were good. And, yes, Brandt was good.

Ed Jones. Not John Cappelletti. Not David Jaynes. Not John Dutton.

On Tuesday, January 29, 1974, the Cowboys made their move official. "I get a knock on my door about 6:00 in the morning, and it's a representative from the Cowboys," Jones said. "And he said, 'You need to be out front at 8:00 AM sharp to take a picture with Tom Landry in front of the billboard welcoming you to Dallas."

Jones didn't believe it.

He was just told the night before from two men he trusted that being the No. 1 overall pick wasn't happening. Then the Cowboys had come to his hotel room door, saying to get out of bed because Landry, his new coach, was waiting for him. "Yes and don't be late," he was told.

Jones said he waited for 15 minutes sitting in his room, trying to process what was happening. He didn't tell anyone what was going to become official in a few hours. Jones walked outside his hotel room and went to the front of the building and saw the billboard. With a white background "Welcome Too Tall Jones" in black lettering sat high above the ground waiting for him.

"I rushed and tell my brother-in-law," Jones said.

Matthews thought he was lying. Jones informed him this wasn't his truth but the truth of everyone. It was real. "Go tell Coach," Matthews said.

Dallas Cowboys coach Tom Landry is dwarfed by first-round draft pick Ed "Too Tall" Jones as they pose together in late January of 1974.

Jones knocked on Merritt's door. The veteran coach was drinking coffee and smoking a cigar. It was his way of relaxing. The best way to start the day on what could be a confusing Tuesday in Dallas.

Merritt opened the door, and here came "Too Tall" Jones, all 6'9" inches of him.

After taking a few puffs, Merritt was told about the billboard, the upcoming No. 1 selection, and that they needed to get to the Cowboys offices at 8:00. "He almost swallowed his cigar," Jones said.

Around 8:00 the trio got to the Cowboys offices and were ushered into a lounge where they had to wait a few moments. Schramm, the Cowboys president, came in and walked over to congratulate Jones. Brandt entered and did the same. Then Jones and his party were taken into an office where Landry was sitting. The head coach told Jones he had a hell of a career at Tennessee State. He shook Merritt's hand and told him he did a great job of coaching Jones. Landry also congratulated Matthews, the man who got Jones into football.

Jones was the No. 1 pick. "Draft time rolls around, and I'm still nervous," he said. "They haven't called my name yet."

The salutations come around 8:00, but the draft wasn't until later that morning. When NFL commissioner Pete Rozelle announced Ed "Too Tall" Jones name as the No. 1 pick, it finally became real. "Gil Brandt walked over and said, 'There's a phone. Call your mom.'"

The No. 1 overall pick from Tennessee State spoke to his mother. He was the first player from a HBCU to be the No. 1 pick in the NFL draft.

Then everyone went outside back to the hotel. A smiling Landry, wearing a sports coat, stood next to Jones. Wearing tinted glasses and a multi-colored dress shirt, Jones seemed stunned. What didn't seem real to Jones was now a reality. The Cowboys tried to tell Jones, but he didn't believe him. He was the No. 1 overall pick.

The No. 1 overall pick of the 1974 NFL Draft played 15 NFL seasons. Jones was a dominant force along the Cowboys defensive line, starting in 203 of 224 games. Jones retired in 1979 to become a professional boxer—only to return the next season. The three-time Pro Bowler was named to the All-Pro team in 1982.

3

HERSCHEL WALKER

THE DALLAS COWBOYS' three Super Bowl titles in the 1990s are attributed to Herschel Walker. He didn't actually play in those three championship games—not in any of the playoff games either. It was the trade between the Dallas Cowboys and the Minnesota Vikings that allowed them to obtain the draft picks necessary to rebuild their franchise. It was a trade so impactful the Cowboys are considered the team of the '90s due to the three titles.

Just before the title run, the franchise was in shambles.

Something had to change, and that's when Jerry Jones and Jimmy Johnson took over. It's not hard to understand how it happened. But it did.

The Cowboys needed players. Well, good players, players who could have an impact on their team. All title teams have luck, good coaching, and players. Some teams get away with average coaching, but there is always a common theme: players. If you don't have talented players who buy into the schemes, everything a coach or an executive is trying to accomplish fails. In order to get those players, Dallas had to pull off one of the biggest trades in NFL history.

It wasn't a complex deal but one that was needed with the Cowboys seeking to escape the plight they were under. Johnson knew the rebuilding of the Cowboys was going to be long. "You don't turn around football teams overnight," the head coach would tell assistant coaches. Johnson would have extensive discussions with his coaching staff about the roster.

This was a new world for Johnson, a successful college coach. In college, recruiting was the lifeblood of a football program. If you couldn't find the right players, a college coach would see an athletic director approaching his agent about a buyout.

The NFL was different in terms of acquiring talent. Veteran players ruled the league. Check that—talented veteran players. You could draft players, but their talent needed to show in two or three years, or an agent would get contacted by an NFL owner about employment. It didn't matter if it was in the draft or in recruiting, Johnson knew where the talent came from for success.

Johnson conducted talks with his staff in the meeting rooms of the Cowboys' practice facility in Valley Ranch, a section of Irving, Texas. When Johnson would take jogs around the practice field with some of his coaches, the roster was on his mind. *How do you fix this? How do you get better? Where do you look? Who should you trade for?*

It was a constant theme as a rookie head coach in the 1989 season. It wasn't hard to talk about rebuilding. It was hard actually doing it.

A purge of the roster was needed. An attitude adjustment was also part of it. The Cowboys were a once-dominant franchise that lost their way. Johnson had to change just the little things. It was as simple as changing the offseason workouts. It was conducted by the strength and conditioning coach. He would check the weights of players, make them run sprints, and that was it. The Cowboys weight room wasn't a room. It was located on the property of the complex with weights and a bench just sitting under the sun. "That's going to change," Johnson said. "We enclosed the weight room, and I required our players to be there five days a week. We worked out on the field three days a week and we lifted weights four days a week. We did some things differently, but that was the only way we knew how to do it."

Johnson came from the University of Miami, where he won a national title. He was the hot college coach when Jerry Jones decided he needed to hire his former college teammate at Arkansas. Before the men linked up with the Cowboys, the franchise lost its way. From 1970 to 1979, the Cowboys made five Super Bowl appearances, winning two titles and reaching the NFC Championship Game seven times. Hall of Famers from Tony Dorsett, Roger Staubach, and Randy White became household names in not only Dallas, but also nationally.

The Cowboys were truly America's Team. It didn't matter if football fans despised the open-air stadium, so God could watch his Cowboys, as it was framed by Texans. It didn't matter if the Cowboys became a show with their cheerleaders and colorful personalities of their players. The Cowboys were a winning product on the field.

That was changing.

Tom Landry, the Hall of Fame coach, had missed the playoffs the last three seasons. In 1988 the Cowboys finished last in the NFC East with a 3–13 record. The franchise was floundering. Losing money was just the start of it. It's been assumed the franchise was losing $1 million a day before Jones purchased the franchise in 1989. Cowboys games were blacked out on local television stations because it was hard to sell tickets. The Cowboys didn't meet the requirement of filling enough seats to avoid a blackout. Why would anyone want to see a franchise that was rebuilding?

Johnson didn't care about the marketing of the franchise. That was Jones' job. Jones also understood the process of making money for a failing franchise but wasn't ignoring how things needed to also change on the field. You can't make money with a poor product. Molded as college teammates at the University of Arkansas, the two men were paired as boss and employee in the NFL—head coach and team owner to make it official. Jones and Johnson or Johnson and Jones were united in fixing a franchise headed to the depths of oblivion.

The Cowboys' fanbase didn't have confidence in either man. Johnson was a surprise hire of Jones' in 1989. In some ways, the maverick ways of Jones off the field were Johnson's own personality on the field. This was Jones' first year as an NFL owner and general manager. Risk is something Jones has talked about frequently in his life as a businessman. He challenged the NFL sponsorship rules and won court cases. Jones knew the NFL was a business that could make not only money for himself, but also for the league. Jones leveraged nearly every penny of his fortune to purchase the Cowboys. He was gambling not only a financial stake, but also a reputation of an Arkansas businessman trying to play with the big boys.

Jones always knew he could play with the big boys in the business world. He thought about buying the San Diego Chargers of the American Football League, but his father talked him out of it. Jones waited for his time. While in Mexico on vacation with family, he saw a newspaper story about the Cowboys being for sale.

When it came to the business of the NFL, he listened to the people who had success. "I have spent a lifetime conferring and talking with people that are substantive or have excelled in the areas that I'm in," Jones said in an interview with Dallas radio station KRLD-FM in October 2020. "That's actually how I do it. And, yes, by the time I finish most days, I'm hoarse, not necessarily from in the weeds of minding the business of the day; it's usually because I've had to call on all kinds of input that from people. And it's amazing how we, as human beings, when I ask, 'Can you get over in our areas that we're interested in or have spent some time in?' It is absolutely amazing how we'll spill it and will tell and will give a doctor's degree from the perspective of our experience. I'm talking human beings...I used to read about people and call them up on the phone and literally go see them and never met them, just to talk to them about how they got to where they got, and they would receive me."

Jones adores the advice he received from Hall of Fame executive Bill Polian and Hall of Fame coach John Madden. He wanted to know what it took to build a football team. He wanted to know what it took to make them work on the field. Finding the right type of players and coaches was the first step. It doesn't matter if you're rebuilding or just trying to repeat as Super Bowl champions. Finding talent was paramount to fixing the Cowboys.

Johnson was also a man of risks but understood in his first year as an NFL head coach that ballplayers, who could make plays, meant everything.

Johnson didn't have enough of them. "Jimmy had a lot of handicaps when we first came in here," Jones said. "By the way, we won the one football game, too. And he was accused by one other coach, for sure, of running, making it look like it was a high school program. But, yeah, I can remember those kinds of challenges. Coach Landry was challenged the year before when he only won three games. So, sure, I can recollect real challenges that we've experienced, and by the way, to those guys' credit, they took that adversity, they made adjustments."

Going into the 1989 season, Johnson had quarterback Troy Aikman, the No. 1 overall pick of that year's NFL draft; a promising, brash second-year wide receiver in Michael Irvin; and some veterans on their last breath as NFL players. There was 13-year veteran center Tom Rafferty, 14-year vet defensive end Ed "Too Tall" Jones, and White, who had Hall of Fame jacket waiting for him upon retirement. Cornerback Everson Walls in year nine of his career also resided on the roster.

Yet the best player on this team was a man in his prime: Herschel Walker.

The Cowboys drafted the running back from the University of Georgia in the fifth round of the 1985 draft. With broad shoulders and a physical running style, Walker was perfect for a run-first team. That was how football was played in the 1980s: run first, ask questions later.

Walker started his professional career for the United States Football League's New Jersey Generals. He became a star in the upstart league that was challenging the NFL. The USFL wasn't afraid to have high-scoring games due to the passing attack. Walker thrived as a runner and a pass catcher. His team wasn't much, but Walker was the star. He wasn't eligible to get drafted by the Cowboys until 1985, but over three seasons, Walker was everything for the Generals.

Then with the Cowboys, Walker had Pro Bowl seasons in 1987 and 1988. At 26 years of age, he rushed for 1,514 yards on 361 carries with five touchdowns in that 1988 season. He averaged 94.6 yards per game and caught 53 passes for 505 yards and two touchdowns in 1988. He entered 1989 the same way he always did, expecting to get the ball and lead the offense.

Johnson had other ideas. So did Jones. Rumors swirled that the Cowboys were looking to trade Walker for a hefty load. Johnson even floated the idea of trading Irvin. Johnson wanted a speed receiver, but Cowboys director of pro personnel John Wooten talked him out of it. There wasn't a need to trade Irvin because he had the toughness the Cowboys lacked.

Jones denied the Cowboys were shopping Walker, but it was clear he was. Johnson knew change was needed, and the current roster wasn't enough. Johnson desired young players who could make an impact within three to five years. Johnson had the quarterback in Aikman but sought more talent. He wasn't totally sold on Aikman either but stuck with the quarterback he once recruited in college.

Walker was talented and had value. He was a veteran player who could push a team to another level. "Jimmy was an outstanding coach," Jones said. "We had some interesting times. Those bad years caused us to sit there, caused us to scratch our head and sit down and say, 'What do we got here that we might could move the needle on?' And looked over [and there] stood Herschel Walker. And, so, that bad year had a big emphasis in us turning around and being open-minded to things like that. Hello, let's use this to look at how not only to be interesting, entertaining, but also productive."

What could you get for Walker? The objective was a lot. It was also about finding the right team that was either a player away or desperate for a star. Numerous teams reached out to the Cowboys about trading for Walker. Even the Cowboys' NFC East rival, the New York Giants, expressed interest. The most serious inquiry came from the Cleveland Browns. The Browns had star fullback Kevin Mack, a two-time Pro Bowl player. But in the 1989 season, Mack was arrested on drug charges, and NFL commissioner Pete Rozelle suspended him for 30 days. Mack would eventually serve a six-month jail sentence for his crime.

So the Browns wanted a big back. The Vikings were in the same mode. In 1988 the Vikings won six of their last seven games for an 11–5 finish. But after they beat the Los Angeles Rams in the first round of the playoffs, a 34–9 loss to the San Francisco 49ers in the NFC Divisional Playoffs ended their season. Minnesota rushed for just 54 yards in that playoff game. San Francisco running back Roger Craig gained 135 yards on 21 carries with an 80-yard run in the fourth quarter clinching the game.

Finding a quality running back seemed vital for the Vikings the next season. There is always a team missing one or two players to reach that next level. The Vikings were that team.

But the Vikings' front office tried to get a running back through the draft. In 1982 it selected Darrin Nelson with the seventh overall pick from Stanford. Of the seven running backs taken in the first round, the Vikings picked Nelson over Gerald Riggs (ninth overall to the Atlanta Falcons), Marcus Allen (10th overall to the Oakland Raiders), and Walter Abercrombie (12th overall to the Pittsburgh Steelers) on the draft board.

Nelson ended up as a below-average running back in comparison to Allen and Riggs. He finished 1985 with a career-high 983 rushing yards on 200 carries and five touchdowns. Over the next two seasons, Nelson did average at least four yards per carry with a career-high 4.9 in 1987. But before that 1987 season, the Vikings wanted an upgrade at running back. So with the 14th overall pick, Penn State running back D.J. Dozier was selected. He was the third running back taken off the board. There were seven running backs selected in the first round, and the Vikings once again found one.

The Vikings had pieces at quarterback in Wade Wilson and wide receiver Anthony Carter. The defense had Chris Doleman, a talented defensive end, to pair with defensive tackle Keith Millard. Safety Joey Browner was also a talented player on the back end. Add Nelson and Dozier, and everything seemed right for the Vikings.

Minnesota finished 8–7 and in second place in the NFC Central. With its two running backs leading the way, Minnesota ended the 1987 season 11th overall in rushing. Nelson gained 642 yards, and the rookie Dozier had five touchdowns but just 257 yards on the ground. It didn't stop the Vikings from advancing in the postseason. They would lose to the then-Washington Redskins, who went on to win the Super Bowl that season, in the NFC Championship Game 17–10.

It left the Vikings believing they were close.

In 1988 the Vikings again finished second in the NFC Central and this time lost to San Francisco in the aforementioned divisional playoff game where Craig ran wild. The Vikings had eight Pro Bowl players on that team—none from the running back position. So while the Cowboys were in a rebuilding mode, the

Herschel Walker would earn two Pro Bowl nods for the Dallas Cowboys, but the assets he brought back in the historic trade were even more valuable.

Vikings were trying to get past elite NFC teams Washington and San Francisco.

Meanwhile, Johnson wanted talented players. Jones knew it, too. But getting them through draft picks was the quickest way to improve. You needed more than six or seven. Johnson thought he needed eight or more picks, young players who could not only challenge veterans, but also other rookies to key the rebuild.

Any serious talks about a Walker trade started with a talk about another player. Wooten called Vikings scout Frank Gilliam to inquire about linebacker David Howard. The two veteran scouts were trying to come up with compensation to present to their respective bosses when Mike Lynn, the Vikings general manager, snatched the phone from Gilliam. "What do you want for Herschel?" Lynn said to Wooten. "What do you want for Herschel?"

"We can't have any shenanigans," Wooten said. "If you are serious about Herschel, I'm going to have to have players and picks."

Walker heard the rumors of a trade but was given assurances by Jones he wasn't going anywhere. He was the Cowboys' best player, and why would you trade the best player on a bad team? "Herschel knew that we wanted to do it," Jones said. "He knew I wanted to do it. Herschel, in my mind, didn't want to leave Dallas. Have you ever tried to trade with somebody that really couldn't care less about where you want to go? Now, that's a hard guy to trade with."

But the Cowboys were planning on it.

Wooten talked to Johnson about the picks, and then the head coach took over. The more picks, the more players, the better. "He's trying to find the best players he could trade, and I guess one was Herschel," Wooten said. "I don't know if he was [serious] about [trading] Michael or not, but it was a consensus. If you do make any trades, got to be Herschel because he's the best thing you got."

To Johnson this was the path. It wasn't clear for him until Lynn took the phone out of Gilliam's hands.

Cleveland, meanwhile, heard about a Walker deal and decided to get involved. Atlanta heard about Walker but instead focused on Irvin. The Falcons knew Johnson sought a speed threat at wideout. Despite Wooten's talk with the head coach about what Irvin brought to a team—toughness and leadership in addition to his skill set of being a good route runner with excellent hands—Johnson listened for an offer.

But the Vikings came on stronger than anyone could imagine.

Johnson's first year as a head coach was a mess. The Cowboys started the first two games at the New Orleans Saints and Atlanta. In the season opener, the Saints beat the Cowboys 28–0. New Orleans dominated the time of possession 44:02 to 15:58. Dallas then would fall to 0–5 with 13 turnovers while getting outscored 146–54. Even with Herschel Walker, the Cowboys were a disaster.

In Minneapolis things were going just okay. The Vikings were 3–2 with the trade deadline approaching in mid-October. What might have been the finality of what the Vikings were feeling about the running attack was a 24–17 victory against the Detroit Lions. In that game Barry Sanders rushed for 99 yards on 23 carries for the Lions. The four running backs for the Vikings that day gained 88 yards.

It was time for a trade.

The Vikings, knowing they failed to obtain quality running backs in the draft and having missed out on talented backs such as Allen and Riggs, had to take their shot. Deep playoff runs push teams further down in the first round, so the opportunity to get an elite player lessens. In the Vikings' case, getting a top-flight running back wasn't going to happen in a run-heavy league when you're selecting in the 20s every season. "From where we were drafting, we weren't going to get a blue-chip running back," Lynn said in a documentary about the Walker trade on ESPN. "We knew that. So the only way to really find a running back was through a trade. It was what we needed."

The question was the price.

Johnson had leverage because of the desperation of the Browns and Vikings, and Lynn and his front office were feeling the pressure to make a deal. A running back was the missing piece to an offense that was pass heavy with Wilson or Tommy Kramer at quarterback. Finding a running back like Walker meant everything to this team.

But there was a problem. "I wasn't going to Minnesota," Walker said. "I was like 'Crap, I'm not going to Minnesota. It's cold in Minnesota.' And Jerry was like, 'Well, what does he want to go to Minnesota? What does he need?'"

Walker liked the warm weather in Texas because it reminded him of home. He was born in Wrightsville, Georgia, a small town of roughly 2,100 people. Dallas, of course, was a big city, not a small town such as Wrightsville, but the weather and the warm feelings he received from people in the state of Texas meant everything to him.

This was not the New York/New Jersey area, where he played professionally in the USFL. Playing in that league was about making money for himself and his family. Walker was the 1982 Heisman Trophy winner from the University of Georgia and had one year of college eligibility left. But he couldn't play in the NFL based on the rules. NFL teams were not allowed to draft players who still had college eligibility left.

The USFL was different. It needed stars to leave college to become professionals and get NFL players on expiring contracts to build their league. So Walker signed a three-year contract with the Generals. The contract was worth nearly $5 million. He wasn't 20 years old when he signed that deal. So learning the business of professional sports came quickly to him.

But with Cowboys and understanding what's at stake for his career, Walker flexed. The Cowboys, while concerned about Walker's feelings about staying in Texas, knew something had to happen. With trade talks picking up with Cleveland and Minnesota, Jones stepped up. Walker had a list. He wanted exit money, a car, and a house. So Jones promised Walker a bonus of $1.25 million, a new car, and a house in Minneapolis that was comparable to the one he had in Las Colinas, Texas.

Walker was good with that. "He really did want to help us out," Jones said. "He thought and he worked to that end. Now, he was a good trader. But at the end of the day, he had everything to do with making it. Right when that was going on, this time of year, my birthday is the 13th."

Yet, more problems arose.

Lynn got tough. On October 11 Lynn told the Cowboys there was a 6:30 PM deadline to agree to trade compensation. Cleveland came strong for Walker. The Browns offered a pair of No. 1 picks in addition to three second-round selections as part of the deal. The Vikings, though, offered more potential picks. So the Cowboys sent Walker and three picks to the Vikings. Minnesota sent five players, three draft picks, and a conditional pick to those five players—should either player get cut before February 1, 1990.

More problems ensued.

Nelson, the 1982 first-round pick, was included in the trade. Nelson didn't want to go. He viewed the Cowboys as a losing organization. He was leaving a playoff contender, a team some believed was close to a Super Bowl title. It didn't matter if that one player who could make this work was going to affect Nelson.

Like Walker, he exerted power. It was something rarely seen in the NFL back in the 1980s. NFL players were told to play and keep their mouths shut. The lack of guaranteed contracts gave NFL owners more power over the players. But here were two players, Walker and Nelson, commanding teams to give them something to make a trade work.

Dallas needed picks to give its rebuilding plan more juice. Minnesota needed Walker to make a Super Bowl run. People were holding it up.

Nelson never really liked playing in Minnesota. He was from Sacramento, California, and attended Stanford where he had a stellar career. In four seasons Nelson rushed for 4,033 yards with 24 touchdowns for Stanford. In the 1981 season, Nelson finished sixth in the Heisman Trophy voting. He rushed for 1,014 yards and caught 67 passes for 846 yards. He combined for 16 touchdowns his final year at Stanford. So picking him in the top 10 wasn't a shock given the success he achieved in college.

Nelson heard about his trade to the new locale. "[Vikings coach] Jerry Burns called me in and told me," Nelson said in an interview with NFL player engagement. "I had no clue until that day. I was pretty surprised to say the least. But what can I do afterward? If you're playing in the National Football League, you have to accept those kinds of things. So I accepted it."

While Walker was certainly a southern gentlemen, Nelson was a Californian. However, Nelson, like Walker, made a power play. "Well, I didn't accept it," he said. "I went to Dallas to kind of check it out because they flew us down there the next morning, but I didn't really feel that I wanted to play in Dallas. I told them that they can either trade me or I would retire. So they traded me to San Diego."

On October 12, the Cowboys finally sent Walker packing to the Vikings. Walker was packing his bags from his house in Las Colinas with the assistance of his agent, Peter Johnson, and Stephen Jones. There was a four-door BMW awaiting Walker as he stepped out from his house on a clear sunny day. He was wearing a dark-colored tie with a white shirt. Walker looked calm as he placed clothes into the trunk of the car.

Stephen Jones looked rushed, knowing his father's private plane was awaiting to fly Walker and Peter Johnson to Minneapolis. Stephen Jones was about to drive Walker to the airport, when a television crew stopped by. "It was a great deal for both parties," Walker said to Dallas television station WFAA. "You can't pick a better team to go to than the Minnesota Vikings. I'm going to miss Dallas a great deal. There's a lot of people I really love and I really respect."

So the trade went down like this: Dallas received a 1992 first-round pick and six conditional picks over a three-year period. There were two first-round picks, three second-round selections, and a third-round pick sent to Dallas. Veteran linebackers Jesse Solomon and Howard, along with cornerback Issiac Holt, defensive end Alex Stewart, and Nelson were traded to Dallas. Nelson was also dealt to San Diego for a fifth-round pick. That fifth-round pick was eventually sent to Minnesota. "One owner said it was the great train robbery," Jimmy Johnson said at a news conference that day as reporters were stunned by the deal. "Whatever it is, we're happy."

The rookie quarterback, Aikman, was surrounded by reporters asking his thoughts on the trade. Aikman wondered aloud why they made the trade. *How do you trade your best player for the unknown?*

Minnesota would get not only Walker, but third- and 10th-round picks in 1990 and a third-round selection in 1991. It was the largest trade in NFL history. There were 18 players involved in the deal.

In 1953 the Baltimore Colts and Browns made a trade involving 15 players. In 1971 Washington and the Rams were in a 14-player deal. Before the 1989 trade, the 1953 and 1971 trades were the largest in league history. It became official on October 13, 1989, when Personnel Notice No. 195-89 was filed with the league office. That date was also Jerry Jones' birthday.

"We were electing a new commissioner, Paul Tagliabue," Jerry Jones said. "And Pete Rozelle, the commissioner at the time, would tell the owners, 'If you don't come to these meetings, you're going to be fined $50,000 for each one of these that you miss.' You'd go to these meetings, and everybody would be sitting around talking. I was visiting with Mike Lynn, visiting with Art Modell. I was visiting about trading Herschel Walker weeks before we ever started directly talking about it. So anybody that has any thinking that it was their unique idea, there were a lot of different ways, a lot of ways of thinking, coming up with Herschel...*Was he the future? What direction were we going to go?* Those kinds of things. The reason I'm saying this is…Jimmy. We didn't have any of this B.S. at that time. Both of us felt so lucky to get up in the morning and be here. We were hemming and hawing and working together, not worrying about who was doing what. I'll tell you this: we had our sleeves rolled up and we were working, doing everything we could to help build this team."

This was a blockbuster.

Once handicapped as a coach with a lack of talent, things would change now for Jimmy Johnson. "The legacy of the trade is it was the beginning of the dynasty the Cowboys had at that time," Walker told *The Dallas Morning News* in a 2014 interview. "I've been asked if I have hard feelings. I don't have hard feelings against anyone."

In some ways, Johnson tries to downplay the trade. He's of the belief—regardless of the picks and players gained in the trade—something could go wrong. Johnson never wanted any of the players from the Vikings. But he did want the picks. The pressure was on him to make the right selections with these draft picks. The players were disposable pieces to the plan.

Of course, the Vikings, despite giving up so much for Walker, were under a different sort of pressure. It was time for them to take a shot at the elite of the NFC. "He wasn't a 1,000-yard guy," Lynn told ESPN. "He was a 1,500-yard guy."

For Johnson the 1989 season would get in the way of what he was trying to accomplish: rebuilding. Fans hate to hear that word; team executives and coaches don't like using it either. But rebuilding was the truth.

Johnson dealt with the truth. "A lot of people point to the Herschel Walker trade and obviously the end result. We got three or four players out of it, but people even today don't understand the trade," Johnson would say years later. "They thought we got five players and five picks. Every player was tied to a pick, and the players Minnesota gave us were all players they could get rid of and not really affect their football team. Jesse Solomon with a bad knee; Issiac Holt, he was an older player; David Howard was an older, try-hard guy. Now as it turned out, we kept those three players, but they weren't part of the Super Bowl run. We made the trade for one reason: the picks."

Johnson made note of the 1987 trade the Rams made with the Indianapolis Colts and Buffalo Bills. That was a 10-player deal involving Eric Dickerson, one of the great running backs in league history, moving from the Rams to the Colts. The Rams got three No. 1 picks from two different teams, and the Bills got the rights to sign Colts linebacker Cornelius Bennett. "Rams had a similar deal with Eric Dickerson," Johnson said. "But the key is not getting picks; the key is picking the right players, and if you pick the right players, that's going to improve your football team. But that was one trade. We made 51 trades in that five-year period."

The aftermath of the trade allowed the Cowboys to select running back Emmitt Smith, defensive tackle Russell Maryland, wide receiver Alvin Harper, cornerback Kevin Smith, and safety Darren Woodson. All key members to the title runs. Smith would become the all-time leading rusher in NFL history. Woodson retired as the leading tackler in Cowboys history.

Johnson's time with the Cowboys lasted five seasons, winning Super Bowl titles in 1992 and 1993. The breakup between Johnson and Jones was one of the biggest sports stories in the 1990s.

Jones said he made a mistake in letting Johnson go. Barry Switzer, the man who replaced Johnson, told Jones this during an interview for the Cowboys job. At the time, giving credit seemed more important than winning titles. Jones and Johnson worked well together to get the Walker trade done. The team they built was so strong that Switzer won the third title in the 1990s in 1995. "Somebody started saying that in the NFL that the ultimate decision maker is not the owner. They need to come read the rules of the NFL," Jones said in a 2014 interview. "If it so happens the GM is the owner, and then you got the coach, then the ultimate decision maker is obvious, and that's by the bylaws of the NFL. So if it came down to a you-know-what contest between me and a coach because of that agreement of something written down or something perceived to have been written down, it's not worth the paper it's written on who makes the call relative to the owner."

All the success in the 1990s was due to the Walker trade.

Minnesota didn't have the same success. The Vikings failed to utilize Walker in a similar fashion. Walker was a running back who could run off the edges and catch passes out of the backfield. Minnesota wanted Walker to run between the tackles.

It never worked.

Walker was a two-time Pro Bowler in six seasons with the Cowboys. He lasted three years with the Vikings with no Pro Bowl berths and just one postseason appearance. The Vikings, a franchise believing it was on the cusp of elite status in the NFC, won the NFC Central in 1989 but lost in the divisional round to San Francisco, the eventual Super Bowl champion. Minnesota missed the postseason in the 1990 and 1991 seasons. "One of the things I learned in life: you never regret," Walker said in an NFL Network documentary. "I don't look back."

Dallas and Minnesota made their decisions for the trade for the right reasons. Fans of the Vikings praised Lynn for the move at the time because there was a belief Walker was the missing piece. As the games grew along with the years, fans believed the trade was one of the worst in NFL history. Vikings fans saw the Cowboys morph from laughingstock to elite status not only in the NFC, but also the NFL.

The Vikings didn't have to rebuild to return to a consistent playoff franchise under new coach Dennis Green in the 1990s. But the Cowboys became elite. They set the standard. It was the start of the dynasty. "The Herschel Walker trade, without question, helped our football team," Johnson said. "It was just a small part of the turnaround with the Cowboys."

The Walker trade started the Cowboys dynasty of the 1990s. The Triplets. Jimmy vs. Jerry. The Cowboys vs. 49ers rivalry. Football in the '90s was fun.

So did Minnesota elevate itself? Not even close. The Vikings misused Walker, thinking he was a between-the-tackles runner, when in reality he could run off the edge and be used in the passing game. In its first year with Walker, the Vikings finished 10–6 in 1989, losing in the NFC Divisional Round. But they didn't make the playoffs the next two seasons with Walker. Burns, the head coach, retired after the 1991 season. Walker would go on to play for the Philadelphia Eagles, Giants, and then returned to the Cowboys for the 1996 and 1997 season to conclude his career.

4

THE TRIPLETS

THE DALLAS COWBOYS took over the NFL in the 1990s. To reach that point, like most NFL teams, heartache was needed. The Cowboys were a franchise that played in five Super Bowls in the 1970s. It was a franchise that won titles in the 1971 and 1977 seasons. The stars of those Cowboys' teams got old. It happens. It's part of the process of playing professional sports. NFL players can only play for so long. The mental and physical toll on a player's body can only take so much in a sport where crashing into another man is acceptable.

That's why you see players in their 30s start to leave. Sometimes those departures are forced when a team releases them or doesn't offer a new contract. It's hard to determine when a player's playing life will expire. A player might have a career year at 29. Does that mean he's ascending? Does that mean he's reached his peak? No team executive, coach, scout, or player can determine this.

When it's time to move on from players, finding replacements in the NFL draft and free agency is the only place. You can't call the human resources department asking for replacements. Instead, replacements are on college campuses and the free-agent market. In the late 1980s, the Cowboys faced this problem.

After winning the NFC East in the 1985 season, the Cowboys were eliminated in the NFC Divisional Round 20–0 by the Los Angeles Rams. It was a pitiful performance by the Cowboys. Quarterback Danny White was sacked five times and threw three interceptions. Tony Dorsett rushed for 58 yards on 17 carries. It was so bad for the Cowboys that with 2:05 left in the contest, coach Tom Landry elected to punt from his own 29. No quest to go for it on fourth down. Rams running back Eric Dickerson set an NFL playoff record with 248 rushing yards on 34 carries and touchdown runs of 40 and 55 yards. "That's not a shabby day," Dickerson told Irv Cross of CBS Sports after the game.

Landry walked off the field alone. There was no security guard with him as he ventured across the field. He looked lost almost as if he wanted to be somewhere else. It appeared he wanted to walk toward the locker room before better judgment prevailed, and he shook the hands of Rams coach John Robinson.

Few teams believe the ending is near after a championship run. But for the Cowboys, this was it. Some of the Cowboys' superstars were in their 30s—that threshold where NFL teams begin to seek younger talent. Tony Dorsett. Ed "Too Tall" Jones. Randy White. Danny White. The end was here.

In 1986 Dallas finished 7–9. There was a 7–8 ending in the shortened 1987 season. Dallas had missed the postseason for consecutive seasons for the first time since 1960–1965. The early 1960s were the Cowboys' inception into the National Football League. After a few years of mediocrity, the Cowboys reached the postseason on a regular basis. It was a franchise that went from expansion to perennial postseason appearance.

But in the late 1980s, the Cowboys entered a dark phase. It was time for a change.

Landry, the only head coach this franchise had ever known, was revered. If it wasn't done in Landry's way, any other way was considered wrong. But Landry had troubles. Tex Schramm, the team president and general manager, and Gil Brandt, the executive in charge of personnel, were going to help Landry get the Cowboys back to the standards they were accustomed to.

It wasn't going to happen in the late 1980s. The franchise needed a jolt of energy. It needed to recover from a period of malaise. It had to return to the NFL draft for talented players.

It's the only way.

MICHAEL IRVIN GREW up poor in Fort Lauderdale, Florida. Being poor was such a relative term in the Irvin household because the love the family had for each other made them feel rich.

The love gave them power. It gave them inspiration.

Irvin was one of 17 children to Walter and Pearl Irvin. Michael Irvin was child No. 15. The Irvins lived in a two-bedroom house on Northwest 28th Avenue where finding a place to sleep was a chore. Irvin said he grew up sleeping four to a king-sized bed. Bunk beds were used as he got older. When they tired of fighting for space on a bed, sleeping on the floor was easier. If you wanted to sleep, you would find a spot.

Michael Irvin lovingly told NFL Films a story when his shoes would get too small that his father would say it's all right. The father cut the top of the shoes and then sliced the front of the shoes so the toes would stick out. If the leather of the shoe was still good, the shoes remained.

Irvin's father, Walter was nicknamed "Rev" because he was a preacher. The father earned money as a roofer, laid down tile, and drove hours to a church preaching the gospel.

Walter Irvin was the man of the house. The breadwinner. When you have 17 kids, there is no choice but to provide for a family. Fight for a family.

But Walter Irvin lost two fights. Instead of stifling the Irvins, it just inspired them. It made the son, Michael Irvin, look at his dad like a superhero. Walter Irvin lost a fight with the Florida High School Activities Association. The other was cancer.

The cancer fight prevented him from seeing how great his son, Michael, was in his senior year of high school and how the fight with the state of Florida was worth it.

There was tremendous potential in what Michael Irvin could do on the football field. He attended Piper High School for two years before a fight during his sophomore year got him suspended. The Irvin family thought the suspension was unjust. It wasn't something they felt was warranted. Irvin was a kid, 16 years old, and young people get into arguments all the time. So not happy with the result of the suspension, Walter Irvin enrolled his son into St. Thomas Aquinas High School. It was a catholic school and, while the transfer was for personal reasons, it didn't sit well with Piper High School and the athletic community in Fort Lauderdale.

Michael Irvin was more than just some kid who played basketball and football. He was a star player. Officials at Piper High wouldn't sign a waiver allowing Michael Irvin to transfer to another school. It bothered Walter Irvin, a baptist preacher with high principles. Yes, Michael Irvin was a star high school player, but this was about more than football. This was about respect and Walter Irvin, the breadwinner in the family, wasn't receiving it.

The community, especially the administrators at Piper High, believed the transfer was about sports. Irvin could transfer to any school he wanted to but would have to sit out the junior year of high school. The father appealed to the Florida High School Activities Association and was denied an approval for the son to play his junior year. Walter Irvin took the case to local courts, and that didn't fare so well. Michael Irvin had to sit out his junior year of high school at St. Thomas Aquinas.

The year didn't derail Michael Irvin. He waited. He worked out. He ran 40-yard dashes in his neighborhood. He was never the fastest kid in the neighborhood, but nobody had the heart he had. The family made sure Michael Irvin worked on his studies during that junior year. And when that senior year started, Rev's next fight arrived: cancer.

During the summer of Irvin's senior year, the Rev, the father, the breadwinner, the rock of the family, was losing that battle. Walter Irvin died of a brain tumor three days before Michael Irvin's first football game at St. Thomas Aquinas.

To say it was devastating to the family wouldn't be the correct way to say what this loss meant. *How do you describe losing a father? How do you describe losing a husband? How do you describe how this feels?* Michael Irvin called his father his hero. He didn't let that loss stop him from becoming a highly sought-after college prospect. When his senior year ended, he committed to the logical school where top South Florida prospects went back in the 1980s: the University of Miami.

It was without any question where Michael Irvin would go. He attended the school not far from home, so family and friends could see him play. The desire to play professionally was becoming more realistic. All Irvin had to do was do his part. In three seasons Irvin set school career records in receiving yards (2,423), touchdown receptions (26), and was second in receptions (143). He was an All-American—whether it was first or second team—in his first three seasons. He was the soul of the Miami football program. His voice was loud. His game was louder. He didn't have blazing speed, but his hands and ability to play a physical brand of football stood out. He was a dominant player when he needed to be. Secondaries tried to stop him, but it was difficult especially when there were big games. A teammate nicknamed him: Playmaker.

All that was left was the NFL draft.

The Dallas Cowboys finished the 1987 season at 7–8 with its best wide receiver being Mike Renfro, who caught 46 passes for 662 yards and four touchdowns. Running back Herschel Walker was the offense. He caught a team-high 60 passes for a team-high 715 yards with one touchdown. Walker was everything for the Cowboys offense. But this was a team that sought more. The NFL draft was going to provide this for a passing offense in desperate need of, well, playmakers.

The top wideouts in the 1988 draft were led by Heisman Trophy winner Tim Brown from Notre Dame. The others were Sterling Sharpe (South Carolina), Aaron Cox (Arizona State), Wendell Davis (LSU), Anthony Miller (Tennessee), and Irvin. It was a strong receiver class in a draft featuring some of the best defensive players in the country, including Neil Smith (Nebraska), Aundray Bruce (Auburn), and Irvin's own teammate, Bennie

Blades, among the top projected picks. Even at Irvin's given position, wide receiver, there were challenges. Brian Blades, a man whom Irvin played youth football against in the same Fort Lauderdale neighborhood, and Brett Perriman were on the same college team. Perriman and Blades were projected Day Two selections.

That Miami team went 12–0 in 1987, beating six ranked teams en route to a national championship. It was the second national title in the program's history. Stacked with elite talent, the roster was confirmation that coach Jimmy Johnson was not only an outstanding recruiter, but also put together a standout coaching staff that could lead the talent on the field to success.

After that ensued the 1988 NFL Draft, while Irvin waited with family and friends in that two-bedroom house in Fort Lauderdale for his chance. Draft experts had Brown and Sharpe as the top receivers. Brown went first (No. 6 overall) to the Los Angeles Raiders. Sharpe was next (No. 7) to the Green Bay Packers. "He was not just in our top five," Tex Schramm said. "He was in the top of our top five. Yes, he was our No. 1."

So who was next? Cox? Miller? Davis? One of the possibilities, Irvin, watched the draft at home. In the late 1980s, prospective draft picks sat at home as the draft was displayed on television on Saturday afternoon from New York. Brown watched it at his apartment until getting a call from Ron Wolf, an executive of the Raiders, saying he was their selection. Irvin had a throng of family and friends watching the NFL draft with him. Television cameras were in tow. He had an earring in his left ear, a chain around his neck, and confidence coming through his pores. He waited for his time. He wanted it. But where?

The New York Giants drafted guard Eric Moore from Indiana at No. 10. Dallas was next.

Irvin received the phone call from the Cowboys saying he was going No. 11. The family celebrated as television cameras taped the entire scene. It was a loving, yet wild environment. Irvin sat with his mother, Pearl, and Aunt Fannie as NFL commissioner Pete Rozelle made the announcement from a ballroom at the Marriott Marquis in New York. "Marshall Irvin" is what Rozelle called Michael Irvin.

It didn't matter that Rozelle got the first name wrong. Everybody knew.

On the backend of his legendary coaching career while trying to push the Cowboys back to greatness of the 1970s, Tom Landry found a talented player nicknamed Playmaker. "He has all the qualities," Landry said. "He's a big receiver, 6'2", 190 pounds. He can run 4.5, and that's really moving for a wide receiver. And he can catch all kinds of passes. He really doesn't have too many weaknesses at all."

Irvin danced in the backyard of his two-bedroom house, the same house he shared with his siblings. He finally arrived. He yelled when the Super Bowl came to Miami, the Cowboys would be there and that he's going to score touchdowns for them.

Despite the praise he gave Sharpe, Schramm knew what Irvin meant: the start of returning the Cowboys back to elite status in the NFL.

When Irvin got to Dallas the day of the NFL draft, that broad smile of his continued for more television cameras when he entered the Irving, Texas, complex. "I'm real excited about it," Irvin said. "Dallas made a commitment to me because knowing my situation I have to graduate before I play football for the Dallas Cowboys."

JIMMY JOHNSON'S RELATIONSHIP with Troy Aikman was like a thorny rose. There will be blood on the palm of your hands, but eventually everything smells good. Johnson, a college coach, pleaded for the coveted high school prospect, and then the college coach asked for Aikman to transfer from Oklahoma to the University of Miami. Each time, Aikman refused his request to play for him. There was a yearning from Johnson for wanting Aikman. It was easy to see why.

Aikman was a California kid. He was born in West Covina, California, about 19 miles from downtown Los Angeles. He played baseball and enjoyed the summer weather where he lived a simple life of sports, friends, and family. Everything changed for Aikman when he entered the eighth grade. The family moved from the sunshine of California and the bright lights of living near Hollywood to the middle of nowhere.

That nowhere was Henryetta, Oklahoma.

Aikman suddenly went from living in suburbia to living on a farm. His father, along with two carpenters, built their one-story home. His mother became a typesetter for a local newspaper. Aikman was growing up on a farm where plowing hay, taking care of horses, and other outdoor chores became the standard. One big difference between California and Oklahoma is the sports. In California, baseball, surfing, track and field, and basketball are the priorities. In Oklahoma, football rules. It's No. 1. It's everything.

You can't say Oklahoma is like football-crazy Texas, but it's a close second to the fanbase and what the sport means to the people living there. There were no pro teams in Oklahoma during Aikman's formative years, but there was the University of Oklahoma. It's a college team, but the fans' passion and interest for the Sooners matched what's typically reserved for pro teams.

Dallas Cowboys quarterback Troy Aikman (right) and wide receiver Michael Irvin celebrate their win against the Pittsburgh Steelers in Super Bowl XXX.

When Aikman was being recruited, the two main state schools wanted him: Oklahoma and Oklahoma State. Johnson was the head coach at Oklahoma State, and Aikman committed to playing in Stillwater, Oklahoma. Aikman, however, wanted to make one more recruiting visit. Johnson didn't want him to go but was helpless.

Aikman visited Norman, Oklahoma. On the school's campus, Aikman noticed the five national championships the football program had won, the number of players that reached the NFL, and that legendary coach Bud Wilkinson, the all-time winningest coach in school history, had 14 conference titles and three national titles on his resume. Aikman committed to Oklahoma and coach Barry Switzer.

In high school Aikman was able to run the option despite the 6'4" frame of a quarterback that seemed better suited for a drop-back passer. Playing for a college program considered a pro team, along with Switzer building a program to compete for national titles, appealed to Aikman.

So Johnson, who thought he had his stud quarterback, was left without him.

But everything changed in 1985. Aikman broke his lower left leg in a 27–14 loss to Miami. At that point Johnson had left Oklahoma State and was morphing that Miami team into a national power. Aikman watched quarterback Jamelle Holieway take over, and OU went back to more of a run-oriented offense where the quarterback was utilized in the option game.

That didn't fit with Aikman. So after the 1985 season, he decided to transfer. Switzer, knowing his quarterback wanted out, called several schools seeking a quarterback. With Aikman being a kid from California, finding a school on the West Coast might have been appealing. It might give him the comfort he sought after being unsatisfied at Oklahoma. Switzer contacted UCLA coach Terry Donahue and said he should take a look at Aikman. In an interview with NFL Network, Donahue expressed surprise at the phone call and the ability to get Aikman for the 1987 season.

Johnson, meanwhile, sought Aikman again. With its talented group of wide receivers and powerful defense, Miami could have used another strong-armed quarterback. Johnson made his second plea. *Come to South Florida. Play with Michael Irvin. Play with Brett Perriman. Play with Brian Blades.*

Aikman said no. He was going home. Sure, Oklahoma was home, too, but the years spent growing up SoCal were a draw for Aikman, and Aikman went to UCLA.

In two seasons he emerged as one of the best quarterbacks in the country. In 1988 Aikman finished third in the Heisman Trophy voting behind the winner, Oklahoma State running back Barry Sanders, and USC quarterback Rodney Peete. When Aikman left UCLA, he had completed 64.8 percent of his passes for 5,298 yards with 41 touchdowns and 17 interceptions. He was the 1987 Pac-10 Offensive Player of the Year. He was an All-American in 1988 and won the Davey O'Brien Award as the best quarterback in the nation. He was set to become one of the top draft picks in the NFL draft.

Meanwhile, the 1988 season for the Dallas Cowboys was a debacle. After a 2–2 start, the Cowboys lost 10 consecutive games. The season had quarterback Steve Pelluer finish the last year of his contract while completing just 56.3 percent of his passes with 19 interceptions and 17 touchdowns. Running back Herschel Walker led the team in rushing with 1,514 yards on a career-high 361 carries. Walker touched the football 414 times in the 1988 season.

To say Walker was a workhorse of this team was an understatement. He was the impetus of what the Cowboys' offense was.

Coaches and players will tell you winning matters. A draft spot means nothing to them in some sense because players and coaches live in the moment. You play the games. You worry about the consequences later. The Cowboys, however, were in a battle with the Green Bay Packers for the No. 1 overall pick toward the end of the 1988 season. The Packers, once a proud franchise like the Cowboys a generation before, started the season 2–5 before a seven-game losing streak sent the season into a collapse.

In Week 15 Dallas defeated the then-Washington Redskins at RFK Stadium 24–17. It seemed that meaningless victory would cost Dallas a No. 1 pick. Then, in the same week the Cowboys knocked off the Redskins, the Packers defeated the Minnesota Vikings 18–6 to improve to 3–12. Entering the regular season finale, Dallas played the Philadelphia Eagles, and Green Bay played the Phoenix Cardinals. A loss for the Packers would give them the No. 1 pick. Dallas lost to Philadelphia 23–7 to conclude the season at 3–13. Meanwhile, Green Bay defeated Phoenix 26–17 for a 4–12 mark. Dallas would pick No. 1, and Green Bay would pick No. 2.

The buildup of the draft centered on the quarterback position and whether the Cowboys needed one. Aikman's final college game came in Dallas at the Cotton Bowl. The Cowboys were an attractive team for Aikman, who expressed a desire to play in a warm climate. Aikman and his teammates were conducting a practice at Texas Stadium during the Cotton Bowl practices.

On television, Texas Stadium looked like a palace. Its hole in the roof so television cameras can look at the football field from above was great for viewers.

But up close, Texas Stadium was a dump. It needed a paint job. It needed luxury suites. It needed more parking spaces. But Texas Stadium was the premier place during the 1970s and 1980s. The stadium was located off the highway in Irving, Texas, which was often misidentified as Dallas by people from outside the North Texas area.

It was home, and Aikman was hoping this would be his new home. Toward the end of one of his practices, Tom Landry attended the session. It prompted Aikman to walk over and speak. Here was the legendary coach, the only coach the Cowboys had known, with a possible new QB1.

Playing quarterback for the Cowboys appealed to Aikman not so much because of the warm weather he would play in during the fall months, but it was, well, the Dallas Cowboys. Don Meredith. Roger Staubach. Danny White. Those were the Big Three quarterbacks in franchise history. Pelluer was the starting quarterback then, but his time was ending, and as the Cowboys tried to restart their drive for another championship, finding a franchise quarterback was needed.

That was Aikman.

At a Cotton Bowl dinner, Aikman sat next to Landry. Gil Brandt, the Cowboys executive vice president, planned to give Aikman's mother and sister a tour of Texas Stadium. It was supposed to be his new home.

If there was any doubt about Aikman, he showed out in the Cotton Bowl during a 17–3 victory against Arkansas. Aikman led UCLA to a then-Cotton Bowl record 19-play scoring drive. He went 12-of-20 on third downs. When it was over, the Bruins gave the Razorbacks their second loss of the season. Aikman completed

19-of-27 passes for 172 yards with one touchdown and one interception. He was also sacked four times.

When Donahue walked up the tunnel to the locker room after the game, he was met by Brandt. According to the *Los Angeles Times*, Donahue told Brandt, "He's all yours now."

Brandt knew who the man was. "He did well," Brandt said. "All those third-down plays and making every one of them. He did everything UCLA wanted him to do and won the ballgame. They didn't have Flipper Anderson or Gaston Green this year, so they really didn't have a lot of speed, which is why they kept throwing short instead of downfield. When you talk about Brendan McCracken, well, he's a good player, but he's a receiver who is a converted quarterback, so they just didn't have much running speed to speak of."

After excelling his senior year, everything seemed perfect for Aikman on the next level. He would play for the Cowboys. He would play for Coach Landry. He would play in a warm weather NFL city.

Perfect.

But Bum Bright, the Cowboys owner, was losing money. He estimated he was losing $1 million a month. Brandt had a tremendous expense account where he would entertain, scout, and make sure the Cowboys' name was continuing its national presence. There was fan apathy. There were financial losses. A change was needed.

Jerry Jones discovered change. He was on vacation in Mexico with family when he read the morning newspaper, a paper from San Diego, that had an item that the Cowboys were for sale. After originally being talked out of buying an AFL franchise by his father, Jones had the money to get after the Cowboys.

He made a phone call to Bright, who didn't know the Arkansas businessman who built his empire through the oil and gas industry. The Cowboys sought someone to save them, and it was Jones. He came in with a brash personality, an Arkansas twang, and $140 million to purchase the franchise.

Bright had some stipulations to the sale.

It was time to let Landry go. The fanbase demanded it, and Bright was willing to do it himself. It was a hard decision, but he didn't want Jones to undergo the scrutiny of firing Landry after just purchasing the franchise. Landry had planned to coach into the 1990s and hired new assistant coaches, including Paul Hackett as the new offensive coordinator to help rebuild the franchise. Landry even had thoughts of coaching an elite quarterback in Aikman.

Jones had other ideas. He fired Landry.

That ending came just a day after he purchased the club on February 25, 1989. Jones, along with Tex Schramm, flew down to Austin, Texas, where Landry had an offseason home. The trio sat together when Jones laid the news down.

Jones was so focused on changing the franchise that he had dinner with Johnson, his former college football teammate at Arkansas, about becoming his new head coach the night before the firing.

Everything just didn't seem right in the NFL with Landry's firing after 29 years. "This is like Lombardi's death," NFL commissioner Pete Rozelle said.

Jones did the dirty work that stunned Dallas. In reality, the firing was necessary, but the process was flawed. Maybe Jones should have given Landry a better send-off and let him coach the 1989 season and have given Landry a chance to push the franchise back to where it once was.

Jones thought otherwise.

The business of the NFL outweighs legends. No player. No coach. No owner. No team executive. No NFL commissioner is bigger than the business of the NFL. Some firings are just unjust, and for many fans, this was. Randy White, the star defensive tackle, said he decided to retire a year earlier than planned. Things were changing around the Cowboys.

One thing that remained was Aikman as the possible No. 1 pick. With Landry gone and Johnson in, a change in philosophy was underway. The Cowboys were going to get younger and wanted as many draft picks as possible to return the team back to what it once was. This wasn't a quick fix, but it appeared that way with the number of deals Johnson wanted to make.

As the NFL draft loomed, Johnson conducted a meeting with his coaches and other front-office personnel. Schramm, the only general manager the franchise had known, was on the way out. He was set to become the president of the new World League of American Football. Brandt, the team executive in charge of personnel, was also nearing a departure. Brandt, however, was hanging on because of his extensive background in scouting elite talent along with his connections to the college game. Barely.

During this meeting Johnson asked people in the room about two players: Aikman and Tony Mandarich. Cowboys scout Jim Garrett wrote lovingly about the UCLA starting quarterback in his draft report. "He very clearly fits the character requirements for the position," Garrett's report said. "He comes into the league better prepared for success than any quarterback I have ever seen."

Garrett's report also said Aikman will miss some passes, and that based on the offense UCLA ran, Aikman threw more shorter passes but had the arm strength to throw downfield.

There was no doubt about Aikman's abilities.

Yet, the Cowboys were getting calls about the No. 1 overall pick.

Packers officials told Aikman he would be their choice if Dallas selected Mandarich.

There was a split in the Cowboys about the two players. Mandarich, a tackle from Michigan State, was a monster. He went from a mid-first round projection to someone at the top of the draft. He took over the NFL Scouting Combine with his size and power. He was measured at 6'6" and 330 pounds. He bench pressed 225 pounds 39 times, ran an amazing 4.65 40-yard on his second attempt, had a vertical leap of 30 inches, and broad jumped farther than 10 feet. *Sports Illustrated* placed him on its cover issue, calling him the "Incredible Bulk" and named him the best offensive line prospect ever. *Ever.*

There were issues with Mandarich away from the field. Steroid use rumors, his lack of awareness for team meetings, and even possible alcohol abuses raised concerns for NFL teams. Mandarich even wanted to challenge heavyweight champion Mike Tyson to a fight before the draft. But the measurables at the Combine almost outweighed those issues.

The Cowboys were one of those teams trying to see if Mandarich was worthy of being a No. 1 pick over Aikman. Johnson polled the room of football experts during a spring meeting at the Cowboys headquarters in Irving, Texas. Jerry Rhome was the Cowboys quarterbacks coach and made an impassioned plea for Aikman. There was no debate. There shouldn't be a debate about Aikman over Mandarich. Johnson along with Jones were settled. It would be Aikman.

The Cowboys didn't wait for the NFL draft to not only draft him, but also sign him to a new contract. Jones opened contract talks with Aikman's agent, Leigh Steinberg, weeks before the draft. With the draft scheduled for Sunday, April 23, 1989, Aikman signed a six-year $11.2 million deal four days before being selected. It was the richest contract for a rookie in NFL history. "I didn't want to take an offensive tackle with the No. 1 pick of the draft," Jimmy Johnson said on ESPN's coverage of the draft. "I want players that could put the ball in the end zone, and we needed a quarterback to build a franchise around, and I had been in Troy Aikman's home when he was a junior in high school and I tried to recruit him for Oklahoma State. When we were at University of Miami, I tried to get him to transfer to University of Miami. I told him, 'You said [no] twice to me. You're not going to say no a third time because I'm going to pick you.'"

Aikman said it was a dream to play quarterback for the Cowboys and especially at the position Staubach made famous. Aikman said he used to watch Staubach play on television growing up in Oklahoma because the Cowboys were the NFL team broadcasted in that part of the country. Now Aikman was going to play for the Cowboys, a franchise in desperate need of a quarterback, considering Pelluer didn't have a contract for the 1989 season.

Johnson finally got his man. "No question in our minds for the simple reasons we've known Troy for a long, long time," Johnson told ESPN. "He's a class individual. He's a very talented individual, and we looked at the long range. We looked at the future of the Dallas Cowboys and what player will have the greatest impact for a long time and we really feel like this year Troy Aikman, without question in our mind, was the player that we needed and the player that could have a positive influence on our club."

The San Diego Chargers, Kansas City Chiefs, and New England Patriots did offer draft compensation to switch with Dallas for the No. 1 overall pick. But in the Cowboys' mind, the first step toward a rebuild started with the quarterback position. Sure, plenty of picks could help and were something Johnson always wanted, but that could be obtained down the line. The first stage of the rebuild was complete: a starting quarterback.

But misery part of any reconstruction of a franchise. Whether it's letting veteran players go in free agency, releasing them, or signing cheaper vets to allow younger players to develop, losses are coming. The 1989 Cowboys went 1–15. That first year under Jones and Johnson meant change was coming, and not everyone was happy.

Just months after drafting Aikman with the No. 1 overall pick, the Cowboys selected University of Miami quarterback Steve Walsh with the second pick of the NFL's supplemental draft. Johnson, a man who praised the drafting of Aikman, and Jones, the team owner who signed the quarterback to the highest contract for a rookie in league history, were confusing people. *Who would be the quarterback of the future?* Aikman went through a terrible season. He suffered a finger injury that allowed him to play in just 11 games. Michael Irvin only played in six games due to a torn ACL.

Then at the trade deadline, the Cowboys made a blockbuster deal in trading their best player, Walker, to Minnesota for what could be the Trade of the Century. At the time of the October trade, Aikman said he wasn't sure of the direction of not only the offense, but also the Cowboys in general. He was playing for a head coach who said that he wanted him for two different schools but then selected a quarterback that helped him win a national title in college. The Cowboys' world looked unfocused. It looked like chaos.

For the inner workings of the Cowboys, it seemed normal. Part of rebuilding a franchise means losses, potential turmoil, and unrest from the fanbase.

Meanwhile, Emmitt Smith was having a year to remember at the University of Florida. The junior running back was finishing his career after three seasons. He broke 58 school records and was named SEC's Player of the Year for the 1989 season. A three-time All-SEC selection and a consensus All-American, Smith, who had quickness and durability, was an expected first-round pick for an NFL team that just needed a running back to complete the rebuild.

But there were problems with Smith. It wasn't his own fault, but his decision on picking an agent gave numerous NFL teams pause. He selected Richard Howell as his agent. Howell wasn't a bad agent. In fact, he was considered very good at his craft. The issue for Smith and Howell was Auburn wide receiver Lawyer Tillman.

In the 1989 NFL Draft, the Cleveland Browns selected Tillman in the second round. The Browns gave up a 1990 first-round pick for the ability to move up in the second round to select Tillman. Howell, who was representing Tillman, said his client deserved to be paid as a first-round pick due to the trade the Browns made. The contract talks were bitter, and Browns executive Ernie Accorsi declared in the summer of 1989 that Tillman wouldn't play that season. "It wouldn't be fair to the other receivers on this team," Accorsi said to reporters at the time. "There are receivers here that have helped us to the playoffs. We couldn't bring him in at a higher salary than them. We're not a 2–14 team looking for a savior."

The stalled contract talks would end, as Tillman played in 14 of the 16 games, catching just six passes. Yet the aftermath soured some NFL teams on Smith, even though it wasn't his fault. He was picking the best possible agent for him.

The Cowboys were in need of talented players on a defense that finished with the fifth worst unit in the NFL. It allowed 24.6 points per game. Dallas was seeking some linebackers to fix its leaking defense. Eugene Lockhart, Jack Del Rio, Randy Shannon, and Ken Norton Jr. were the main linebackers in the 4-3 defensive front. Jesse Solomon and David Howard were rotating linebackers. Upgrades were needed.

At running back Dallas was trying to piece things together. Paul Palmer led the Cowboys in rushing with 446 yards while playing in just nine games. Aikman was the second leading rusher with 302 in 11 games. The running game needed help. So in free agency, then called Plan B, the Cowboys signed running backs Keith Jones and Tommie Agee. So maybe Dallas was getting settled at the running back position.

Meanwhile, there was a growing desire to draft for defense. Cowboys officials fell in love with Baylor linebacker James Francis. A three-time All-Southwest Conference selection, he made 344 tackles at Baylor and blocked an NCAA-record eight kicks in 1989. "He's a can't-miss if that's a possibility," Dick Mansperger, the Cowboys director of scouting, told the *Star-Telegram*. "I would like to have him not miss here."

James Francis' older brother, Ron Francis, was a defensive back on the Cowboys roster. The Francis brothers grew up Cowboys fans while growing up in East Texas. Everything seemed perfect.

Johnson certainly knew about Smith. As the coach of the University of Miami, Johnson watched Smith run wild for the in-state rival. He knew Smith didn't have blazing speed, but his quickness through the holes and physical toughness enabled him to emerge as one of the top running backs in the country.

Smith was a legend in high school. Growing up in Pensacola, Florida, he attended Escambia High School and was named Player of the Year by *Parade* and *USA TODAY*. He finished his career with a state record 8,804 yards on 1,144 carries. He helped Escambia win back-to-back state titles and set a national record with 45 100-yard rushing games. He continued his rise through college at Florida and was ready for the NFL after three seasons.

Three days before the NFL draft, the Cowboys made a trade for a running back. Dallas gave up second- and third-round draft picks to the San Francisco 49ers for running back Terrence Flagler, a first-round pick from the 1987 draft class. So the running back position seemed out.

Outside of the trade for Flagler, the Cowboys fielded a phone call from the Pittsburgh Steelers. Tom Donahoe, the Steelers general manager, called John Wooten, the Cowboys director of player personnel. Wooten helped the franchise in the 1970s and was a calming influence when Johnson worried about the Walker trade in 1989.

Dallas wanted to move up from No. 21 to No. 17. Steelers coach Chuck Noll didn't want to make a deal until the day of the draft. The Atlanta Falcons wanted a trade that included Irvin. But as he did earlier in the 1989 season, Wooten convinced Johnson not to trade Irvin, who he saw as a future star.

The day of the draft saw Smith fall. He thought the Tampa Bay Buccaneers were going to select him with the fourth overall pick.

Dallas Cowboys running back Emmitt Smith runs for some of his 152 rushing yards during a victory against the Los Angeles Raiders in October of 1992.

Schramm, the longtime Cowboys executive, thought Dallas was going to select James Francis. Schramm called Francis and told him it looked good that he was coming to Dallas.

The Chicago Bears indicated to Francis he was going sixth overall to them. "Be patient," Schramm told Francis over the phone.

However, the Los Angeles Raiders called asking Wooten about a deal. "We have put out some feelers about moving up," Wooten said.

The Raiders and Cowboys couldn't get close. So Dallas traded with the Steelers instead, moving from No. 21 to No. 17.

But something else happened. While improving the defense was a high priority, another team stepped in front of the Cowboys. "It looks like you're a Bengal now," Schramm said to Francis.

It was a stunning blow to the ego of Schramm who thought getting this linebacker was important. But once again, the left hand doesn't know what the right hand is doing. Unless, Schramm was just playing coy with Francis. The Bengals, a team that didn't even work out Francis, selected him No. 12 overall. Francis' dream of playing for the Cowboys was over. "It's funny how it worked out," Francis said years later on Sic'Em365, a Baylor radio show. Later in the interview, Francis said, "It would have been great [to play for the Cowboys]. My brother played there. I would have gotten to play [with him]. Who knows what would have happened? My family is Cowboys fanatics."

So Dallas, while trying to trade up for Francis, failed to get him. Then it was time for the Cowboys to select at No. 17. "I didn't know what was going to happen," Smith said in a 2017 interview with Graham Bensinger. "I started to get very nervous because I wanted to go in the top 10, then I fell back to the 17th pick and, by the time the Cowboys made the trade, I got a call from Jimmy."

Dallas picked Smith at No. 17 overall. It was a stunner, considering what the Cowboys wanted to accomplish on defense. "We tried to trade up for defensive help," Johnson said, "with three teams. The defensive ability of the players left on the board didn't warrant a starter. So we went for a quality offensive talent."

The trade that shook up the NFL and is the standard for all other blockbuster trades not only in football, but also all of sports, led to three Hall of Fame players in Aikman, Smith, and Irvin. They produced three Super Bowl titles, which cemented the Cowboys dynasty in the 1990s. After starting his career 0–11 in 1989, Aikman surged as one of the great quarterbacks in franchise history. Aikman doesn't have overwhelming numbers due to the impact of the running game in the 1990s, but he threw for more than 3,000 yards five times, and Smith finished his career as the NFL's all-time leading rusher (18,355 yards), led the NFL in rushing four times, and led the league in touchdowns three times. He scored 46 touchdowns over a two-year span (1994 and 1995). Smith was named NFL's MVP in the 1993 season. Incidentally, Smith held out for a new contract, something that lasted two games into the regular season. Smith became the highest paid running back in NFL history when he returned. After missing two games, Smith not only earned the league MVP, but also led the league in rushing, and the Cowboys won a Super Bowl that season.

Irvin was the soul of the Cowboys. No doubt. He had numerous off-the-field issues, leading to a suspension and fines, but when on the field, Irvin, nicknamed "The Playmaker," was dominant. A physical receiver he was a five-time Pro Bowler, whose career was cut short at 33 years of age, when after suffering a neck injury, it was discovered he was born with a narrow spinal cord. Irvin played football at all levels without any doctor's examination discovering the abnormality. It didn't stop him from reaching a dream of playing in the NFL and contributing to three Super Bowl titles.

5

RANDY MOSS

TANGIE ELLIS DIDN'T pay much attention to it. She was attending the University of North Carolina and also working as a cashier at Food Lion, a grocery store in Chapel Hill. Ellis was married to Greg Ellis, a dominating football player. Still, Tangie Ellis wasn't paying attention.

How could she?

Tangie Ellis was used to her man playing football even in high school, where they met. Tangie and Greg attended East Wake High School in Wendell, North Carolina. A courtship began, and soon they were boyfriend and girlfriend. It still didn't register with Tangie Ellis, then Tangie Love, even when her boyfriend accepted a scholarship to play college football at North Carolina. The high school sweethearts soon became husband and wife. Tangie, the cashier and college student, and Greg, the football player and college student.

Greg Ellis was excelling in a sport that wasn't No. 1 in his home state. The state of North Carolina is a basketball state.

Duke–North Carolina is a bitter basketball rivalry. Michael Jordan. Coach K. Dean Smith. Grant Hill. Bobby Hurley. Roy Williams. Christian Laettner. Phil Ford. These are men who made the rivalry in the modern era. Of course, Duke–North Carolina basketball goes deeper than just these two schools. It brings in N.C. State. Jim Valvano. David Thompson. Thurl Bailey. Tom Gugliotta. Lorenzo Charles. Spud Webb. Those are household names from the No. 3 school in the Carolinas.

Yet, football players excel from this state, whether homegrown or transplants. The most famous is Lawrence Taylor, a Virginia native who went to North Carolina and at that time in the late 1990s was the school's most famous football player. Greg Ellis wasn't trying to be famous. He was just trying to play football.

Tangie Ellis was caught up in working and going to school and not understanding what was going on. So Tangie was going about her day, just working when a vendor approached at the Food Lion and told her, "You're going to be a millionaire."

Tangie was stunned. "What are you talking about?" she told the man.

"Your husband is…he's going to the NFL," the vendor told Tangie.

Where was this coming from? Yes, Greg was a good football player. *But a millionaire?*

Maybe Tangie subconsciously suppressed what was in front of her.

Tangie didn't believe the vendor, who was a big sports fan and followed Greg Ellis' football exploits in college. "And so she just kept on working at the grocery store," Greg Ellis said of the encounter his wife had. "And my mom, they don't keep up with sports on that level."

Somebody was keeping up with sports on that level, and you could add North Carolina football coach Mack Brown to the list. One of his best defensive players was Ellis.

In 1996 Ellis finished his junior season with 62 total tackles, 18 tackles for loss, and 12.5 sacks. The sacks were the third most in a single season in school history. Brown was worried Ellis was going to forgo his senior season and enter the NFL draft. It wasn't about Ellis becoming a rich man by turning pro; it was more about losing a key member of his football team. A team captain, a player well-respected on the roster. Brown knew the NFL was a lure for his players, especially if they could secure a high draft choice. It's important not only for the player, but also for the program as well.

Yet, Brown had to know. The questions needed asking. *Was Brown going to lose his best pass rusher? Did Brown need to find a pass rusher during the recruiting trails a year before he was ready to do so?* "They called me into the office," Ellis said. "Donnie Thompson was my position coach and spoke to me about. I don't know if Mack even remembers this 'cuz he and I never spoke about it. Even when we see each other, we don't speak about it. But I know. My position coach pulled me into his office and he said, 'Man, Brown thinks you're going to leave school early. Are you going to leave?' And I was like, 'No, no. No, I'm not leaving early. I'm staying here longer.'"

The conversation took place during the middle of Ellis' junior season. That's how worried the head coach was. It was also confirmation to Ellis of his future. Whether his wife knew about it, believed it, or ignored it, the NFL was a reality. "But once you conceptualize you can do it," Ellis said, "that's when it kind of started to click for me and come together that I was going to be drafted."

Brown was speaking with NFL scouts and personnel people about the team he had in Chapel Hill. "He was like, 'One day Greg is going to make a whole bunch of money at playing football,'" Ellis said.

Once the season ended, UNC finished 10–2, beating West Virginia in the Gator Bowl setting up an exciting 1997 season.

Ellis' senior year was just as good as the previous one. He had 87 tackles, 18 tackles for loss, and nine sacks. He broke the school record for sacks in a career. As for the team, it was a signature victory when North Carolina knocked off Clemson on the road. It was North Carolina's first victory in Death Valley since 1980. Ellis stuffed the box score with 14 tackles, two tackles for loss, and two sacks. The only loss for the Tar Heels that season was a 20–3 defeat to Florida State. The season wasn't a disappointment as North Carolina finished 11–1, knocking off Virginia Tech 42–3 in the Gator Bowl.

Ellis finished his career with a defense that finished No. 2 in the nation his junior and senior seasons. He was a three-time, first-team All-ACC selection and a two-time All-American.

Ellis was part of an excellent defense with potential first-round picks in defensive tackle Vonnie Holliday and linebacker Brian Simmons. Ellis had the resume to go with skills that could rush the passer with power and finesse. Ellis' long arms gave him the ability to reach left tackles quicker so he could control the line of scrimmage. "You start to appear in the magazines as one of the top players in the country and all that kind of stuff," Ellis said. "I just kind of felt like, *Okay, I don't know if I'm that good, but apparently these people do.* So, I'm supposed to be able to get it done at the next level."

Ellis had believers outside of his inner circle of his family that becoming a star NFL player was real. His junior and senior seasons told them so.

What was next was showing NFL teams at the NFL Scouting Combine that his measurables—the height, weight, speed—and power on the field now in what some NFL coaches called the "Underwear Olympics" were NFL ready. Ellis would play in the Senior Bowl and East–West Shrine Game; he could play against top-level competition, too. Those were opportunities to showcase his skills. Ellis was ready for the challenge. What that vendor that told Tangie about an NFL world in their future was becoming real.

Meanwhile, Randy Moss was just trying to get out of Rand, West Virginia, and get away from the mentality of the people.

He was a talented football, basketball, and baseball player at DuPont High School from nearby Belle, West Virginia. Moss was raised by a single mother, Maxine Moss, with his two siblings. Rand was a small town with a population of under 2,000 on a good day. Moss had a long frame, speed, and smarts to beat defensive backs one on one in football. He could run the floor fluidly in basketball and catch passes for easy dunks in transition. Throw an alley-oop toward the rim, and Moss would go get it. Moss played center field in high school, running down deep fly balls by taking long strides toward the fence. He was a sprinter on the track. He ran the 100 meters, 200 meters, and sprint relays. Moss used those long legs to eat up the track to dominate.

Moss was it.

He was considered one of the top athletes in the state of West Virginia, whose most famous son was Jerry West from Chelyan, West Virginia. West was a legendary basketball player and team executive. He was nicknamed "the Logo" because, well, the NBA logo was created from his likeness.

Moss was morphing into that kind of an elite talent. But Moss was from an area that didn't see beyond West Virginia. There were talented athletes from Rand and from nearby communities, but all they saw after high school was working at the local 7-Eleven, hanging out at the 7-Eleven, or working at a grocery store. Or just hanging out. Or just smoking and drinking.

Playing Division I football or basketball didn't seem realistic. The high school team was the pros. Rand was nicknamed Rand University. You got a master's degree from Rand by hanging out on the street corner.

Moss was being told he was different. If he could earn a scholarship by playing football, he could escape the lifelessness of Rand.

NFL teams explore every draft prospect. They want to know how and why a draft prospect acts the way he does. When the Dallas Cowboys were doing research into wide receiver Dez Bryant in 2010, they sent Larry Wansley, who was in charge of security and investigations, to Bryant's hometown of Lufkin, Texas. One day Wansley sat at a local eatery in Lufkin, and the waitress asked if he was there to find out who Bryant was. It's no secret what NFL teams do. It's finding the secrets that's the hard part. Regardless of how short or long an investigator resides in a town, building trust with a community is important.

Moss' investigations were public record. Going deeper into his attitude and finding the source of his anger was bigger than anything needed. When Moss was eventually an NFL draft prospect, Rand University and Belle became the center point of everything.

It gave you the reasons why Moss was the man he was.

The official date was March 24, 1995, when Moss' life changed. Where the narrative of who he was and what he was became a birthmark on his soul. In an ESPN documentary about his life, Moss talked about racial tension while attending high school. He got into three fights over racial issues in all three years in high school. Moss just couldn't go to school, pass his classes, play sports, and go home. He went to school. He went to class. He played sports, but then he endured racism.

His mother, Maxine, told him never to back down. Be respectful but never back down.

"There was a lot of racial tension," Moss said in the ESPN documentary. "But I didn't understand the magnitude of it."

Later he said, "it was kinda overwhelming to me that I didn't understand it."

How could a 17 year old understand racism? All Moss knew was that he was tired of it.

His telling of the events to NFL teams during the draft process was either ignored or never understood. The pressures of trying to play in college, becoming the star athlete and a young father were tremendous. And then you added racism to the mix.

There was an area inside the school, a hallway to the gym outside the cafeteria nicknamed "Redneck Alley." It was where racial taunts were shouted by White high school students to Black high school students. How could a Black person live through that? Why would you live through that?

Moss' friend sat in a classroom on this March day and had enough. A White student named Ernest Roy Johnson wrote on a desk, "All N-----s must die."

Moss' friend, identified by *The Washington Post* as Rayeshawn Smith, wanted to fight. Smith asked Moss to back him up because when school ended he was going to fight Johnson.

Enough was enough.

Was fighting the answer? For Smith and Moss, the answer was no.

After school on March 24, 1995, Smith beat Johnson senselessly with Moss watching. With Johnson lying on his back, Moss added his two cents. He stomped Johnson twice. Johnson was taken to the hospital in an ambulance with injuries to his spleen and kidneys. Television stations were outside the school showing Johnson being carted off wearing a neck brace before getting lifted into the ambulance. It also showed Moss being arrested for the attack.

The pressures of playing sports, going to class, having a baby, and now racism wore on Moss. "They were done with me," Moss said, "tired of me. Basically, I had a lot of anger built up in me about what I was going through. I was in the paper, people were talking about me. I had coaches recruiting me so I had the notoriety, but at the same time, I had to go to school and deal with this racism. So a lot of my problems of me getting [into] trouble had to do with trying to express what I was going through, and no one listening to what I was going through."

The fight set up Moss' life in an out-of-control state where he lost two Division I scholarships to Notre Dame and Florida State.

The fight.

The aftermath of it just gave people confirmation of what they thought of Moss but not why or what he did.

Could it have been handled differently? Yes. No. Maybe.

How does an NFL team evaluate that?

The fight laid the groundwork for how NFL front-office personnel also felt about Moss.

He was arrested and charged with malicious wounding, a felony that was pleaded down to two counts of battery. He was expelled from high school and had to finish his studies at an alternative school. Smith wasn't charged because he was a minor. But Moss was 17, an adult. He was led into the courtroom wearing an orange jumpsuit and shackles on his ankles.

The 1994 West Virginia High School Player of the Year, who signed a letter of intent with Notre Dame, was now without a football program. Notre Dame rescinded his scholarship. Feeling poorly about the decision made by his school, Notre Dame coach Lou Holtz asked friend Bobby Bowden at Florida State to take Moss. Bowden took Moss quickly.

As part of Moss' agreement with the courts, he would serve three days in jail and finish the remaining 30 days after his freshman year at Florida State. It seemed everything would get back on track for Moss. His life as a bum was not going to happen. He was good. He wasn't allowed to play football at Florida State. He could only practice his freshman year. For Moss that was perfect. He was in Tallahassee, Florida, the state capital, doing what he loved.

Moss never forgot where he came from because how do you forget that. But Moss needed to do something else with his life, and Florida State was providing him with an opportunity. Moss proved himself worthy of playing Division I football. His 40-yard time was the second fastest in school history, trailing only Deion Sanders. Moss left Tallahassee and headed back to Belle to complete his sentence and move on with his life.

Moss smoked some marijuana upon returning to Belle. When he took a court-ordered drug test, he failed it. So a judge revoked his probation and sent him to jail for seven days. Moss was in solitary confinement.

In May of 1996, Moss stood in front of a judge, asking for forgiveness. He apologized to the court and admitted his own mistakes. "Your honor, there is really no need for a hearing," he said. "I'm guilty of smoking marijuana. And the lockdown was really just somewhere I could get away and think about what I've done. And just to see about what do I really want to do with my life. Do I want to be a thug and stay in the jail? Or do I want to be and become a real gentleman and to live my life in a real way?"

Florida State canceled Moss' scholarship, so a potential redshirt freshman year was not happening. Moss sent a video from jail meeting room to his Florida State teammates apologizing and asking them to keep following Bowden.

On August 5 Moss cried in court and was sentenced to 60 days in jail instead of serving a year. But the judge gave him time served, and he was released. It was another chance for Moss.

And another chance for NFL teams to determine what to do with Moss if he could get to college.

THE DALLAS COWBOYS were the team of the 1990s. The franchise won three titles in four years under two different coaches. Jimmy Johnson turned the franchise around with back-to-back titles in the 1992 and 1993 seasons. Johnson's feud with owner Jerry Jones turned the franchise upside down. A breakup was fostering for years. It finally came to a head at the NFL owners' meetings when Jones told reporters he could find anyone to replace Johnson.

He eventually did in Barry Switzer, a legendary coach at Oklahoma. Switzer won a Super Bowl title with the Cowboys, ending the 1995 season. On the podium where he received the Super Bowl trophy, Switzer yelled at Jones, "We did it our way, baby. We did it."

The Dallas Cowboys could've drafted Randy Moss in the 1998 NFL Draft. Instead the rookie burned them for a 56-yard touchdown in the third quarter of the Minnesota Vikings' Thanksgiving Day win that same year.

Jones seemed to ignore Switzer and took the trophy and raised it up high. Jones and the Cowboys were of the belief another title was coming.

If anything, though, it was the beginning of the end of the famed Triplets. But when you live in that moment, you just don't see the ending coming. Jones felt the franchise was in good shape. But cracks to the foundation of the franchise were beginning to show. Off-the-field issues were gaining more attention than the football field.

In April of 1995, just months after winning a Super Bowl title, offensive tackle Erik Williams was charged with sexually assaulting a 17-year-old topless dancer. Williams was cleared of the charges. In March of 1996, wide receiver Michael Irvin was arrested on a drug charge. He was eventually suspended for the first five games of the 1996 season. The court case involving Irvin was a spectacle. During one of his court appearances, Irvin showed up wearing dark sunglasses and a full-length mink coat. Irvin received probation for the drug charges.

Williams and Irvin were charged with sexual assault in January 1997. The alleged victim recanted the charges, and police cleared Williams and Irvin of any wrongdoing. The two players won a defamation suit against a Dallas-area television station for their reporting of the incident.

The Cowboys were a team of bad boys, who partied at a home near their practice facility in Irving, Texas. That house was called the White House for its exterior color.

An NFL team can only go through so much off-the-field drama because it can bleed dangerous things on the field.

In the 1996 season, the Cowboys finished 10–6 after defeating the Minnesota Vikings in the NFC wild-card round but were beaten by the Carolina Panthers 26–17 in the divisional round. Still, Jones believed his franchise could obtain another title.

But the 1997 season ended badly with a 6–10 finish for the Cowboys. The off-the-field issues with the Cowboys players even struck Coach Switzer. As he was headed to the Cowboys' training camp complex in Austin, Texas, Switzer was arrested for carrying a gun in his carry-on bag as he went through airport security. Switzer said he forgot the gun was in his bag, citing a need to keep it away from a child that visited his home. Jones fined Switzer a then-NFL high $75,000 for the incident. "I hope that the actions that I'm taking will be a reinforcement to our fans and to everyone involved that we are working toward a long-term and not a short-term effort to," Jones told the Associated Press, "create more awareness to our responsibility."

With nearly four weeks left in that 1997 season, Switzer pled guilty to a misdemeanor for having a loaded, unlicensed .38-caliber handgun. The Cowboys were trying to move on from their image as an out-of-control franchise. It was difficult. So Jones fired Switzer and hired Chan Gailey as coach once the 1997 season ended.

As the Cowboys were going through turmoil, Randy Moss was thriving. He lost two scholarships—from Notre Dame and Florida State—but found a new home at Marshall.

During the recruiting process, Moss promised his mother he would visit just three schools. The NCAA allowed for five visits, but Maxine Moss was in charge of the recruiting. Moss took three visits: Notre Dame, Tennessee, and Florida. Moss was also interested in Ohio State but didn't make a trip.

Moss, of course, committed to Notre Dame, but his own issues off the field cost him that scholarship, and a failed drug test after completing his freshman year at Florida State left him without a school to attend. One of the biggest problems Moss had in his recruiting was the number of schools that didn't want him. Of course, schools respected the talent, but how could a coach or an athletic director encourage the decision to bring a player who got into a racial fight and failed a drug test to their campus?

The lack of compassion for Moss' issues was glaring.

At times, during the recruiting process, Moss stuck his nose up at state schools. Staying home was not meant for him in his mind. He was from Rand, West Virginia, a place where few people escape from to greater heights, particularly in sports.

One of Moss' closest friends and teammates in high school, Bobbie Howard committed to Notre Dame. "I haven't really ruled anything out, but I doubt very seriously, I'll stay in the state," Moss said before he committed to Notre Dame.

Then after several stints in jail, embarrassing moments where he cried in a courtroom while being led into a hearing in shackles wearing an orange jumpsuit, Moss was humbled about his state. He needed someone to give him a chance.

Bob Pruett had recruited Moss when he was the defensive coordinator at the University of Florida. Pruett was from Beckley, West Virginia. Pruett knew about Rand. He knew about the small towns and thought processes of people from the small towns in West Virginia. Pruett enjoyed West Virginia. But he couldn't convince Moss to stay home.

Pruett then became the head coach at Marshall. Located in Huntington, West Virginia, the school was Pruett's alma mater. He played running back and tight end at Marshall from 1962 to 1964. Marshall was moving from Division I AA to Division I A.

It was a wonderful opportunity for Pruett because he was going home to coach. He was going to take Marshall into a place it had never gone before. The University of West Virginia was the Division I A football program. It set the standard in the state. Marshall was the little brother that couldn't compete with West Virginia. The University of Pittsburgh was the so-called rival for West Virginia football. Not Marshall.

Pruett was hoping to change that.

So in August 1996, Pruett came after Moss. The lure was to play at home for Moss. The lure was to play right away at Marshall. And, of course, the next year, Moss could play Division I A.

Battered mentally from the negative media attention he received and emotionally spent from his own self-inflicted problems, Moss decided it was the right decision. He had nothing to lose. Pruett was looking for a spark of a Marshall program. So in that 1996 season, Marshall started Moss, who wore No. 88.

Marshall dominated the competition in its final year in Division I AA, and Marshall finished with a 15–0 mark. In the I AA title game, Moss took over with nine catches for 220 yards and four touchdowns. He finished the season, setting freshman records in catches (78), yards (1,709), and touchdowns (28).

The talent many saw in Moss was finally on display. All that was needed was another productive year. In 1997 Moss had another strong season, becoming the first football player to place the state of West Virginia on a national stage. He won the Biletnikoff Award as the nation's best wide receiver. He finished fourth for the Heisman Trophy award. Everything Moss lost had now been regained. He became an elite talent with NFL teams salivating to draft him.

Maybe.

The NFL draft process is complex.

Moss was at the top of that complex mess. Here was a talented player that had off-the-field issues. The majority of these off-the-field issues stemmed from high school, where a racial fight began a downward turn that he finally solved. Yet, in his sophomore year at Marshall, Moss was charged with domestic abuse in an incident with his child's mother. Moss admitted to putting his hands on Libby Offutt, his daughter's mother. The charges were dropped, but it was a stain on Moss' record. Just another one on a long list.

It scared NFL teams. "We've had discussions, and Randy Moss is not on our draft board," Bobby Grier, who was the New England Patriots vice president of player personnel, told *USA TODAY*. "Quite a few players are off our board because of character issue."

Everything Moss did was scrutinized—even the sunglasses he wore during the Heisman Trophy presentation. "It gave me a comfort level that everything was A okay," Moss said of why he wore them.

There was no disputing how powerful Moss was on the field. Moss elected to skip the NFL Scouting Combine due to dental surgery. The objective was for Moss to conduct two workouts for scouts. During his Pro Day, Moss did everything that was necessary. He ran the 40-yard dash in 4.25 and 4.38 seconds. There was a vertical jump of 47 inches. He was a 20-year-old man measuring 6'4" and 215 pounds. The No. 1 wide receiver in the NFL draft. Everything seemed right for Moss.

Meanwhile, Greg Ellis had finally taken football seriously—at least the part about getting drafted. The defensive end from North Carolina was invited to play in the East–West Shrine Game and the Senior Bowl. Ellis had a friend question why he would attend

Greg Ellis, who rushes the passer during a 2007 victory, represented a safer choice than Randy Moss in the 1998 NFL Draft.

the East-West Shrine Game. "I mean, I love football," Ellis said
he told a friend. "They invited me to come. So I enjoyed it and
I went."

There were questions about Ellis' weight. The height wasn't
a problem because he was 6'6". At the East-West Shrine Game,
he was listed at 275 pounds. If Ellis was going to play defensive end in the NFL, gaining more weight was important. Some
NFL teams looked at him as a speed rusher, someone to get after
the quarterback in a scheme where he could come off the edge.
Ellis' weight deterred some teams from believing he could handle
double teams because he wasn't 300 pounds.

But Ellis showed off at the Combine. The goal of lifting 225
pounds numerous times is to showcase strength and toughness.
When it gets difficult to lift 225 pounds several times is where NFL
teams want to know just how bad you want to lift these weights.
Ellis laid down on a weight bench at the Combine in Indianapolis,
just trying to bench press 225 pounds. He didn't have a specific
number in mind when it came to lifting; he just understood the
higher the number, the better. "I had a question mark," Ellis said.
"Some people wondered if I was a tweener. *He's a little undersized
to play with power in the NFL.* Especially in those days. Now a
lot of these men are smaller and they play that speed rush end.
But when I came out in that class, they were saying, 'He's a little
undersized and may not be strong enough to start as a rookie in
the NFL in the role of defensive end.' But they also said I didn't
have the true experience to play linebacker either. And so I got
up to do my 225 and I tell you it was a blessing."

Ellis bench pressed 225 pounds 26 times. "So somewhere
around there, it kind of shocked the scouts," Ellis said.

Andre Patterson was the defensive line coach for the Vikings on the day defensive linemen were asked to lift 225 pounds. He asked Ellis if he was looking to reach 26 times on the bench press. "I didn't realize how many [reps]," Ellis said. "But I played it off like, yeah, sure."

When Ellis departed the Combine, he ran a 4.87 40-yard dash in addition to showcasing a 35.5-inch vertical jump. Ellis had the resume produced during his career in college to indicate he could play in the NFL. He also aced the workouts, passing them without further questions. He answered the question if he could play a power game as a pass rusher. He answered the question if he should remain a defensive end despite being light weight-wise.

NFL teams can draft for need or the best player available. Some teams reach for a player because of need, and it ends up hurting that franchise eventually. At Ellis' position the best defensive linemen were: defensive end Andre Wadswoth (Florida State), defensive end Grant Wistrom (Nebraska), defensive end Jason Peter (Nebraska), and defensive tackle (and Ellis teammate) Vonnie Holliday (North Carolina). Ellis was included in this list.

Ellis visited numerous teams, including the Cowboys. The Cowboys front office brought in several draft prospects and had them stay at a Marriott hotel near the airport. All the players would visit the Cowboys' facility in Irving, Texas, to tour the building and meet the coaches and, of course, Jones.

Another prospective draft pick who visited the Cowboys facility in the Valley Ranch section of Irving was Moss. Unlike some of the other prospects, Moss had a different visit. Yes, Moss toured the facility and spoke with Jones, who told all the draft picks that the Cowboys wanted to select him, but there was something else: Moss visited the home of cornerback Deion Sanders.

The Cowboys were going through an emotional time with so many issues away from the field. Sanders even spoke to Irvin about his own struggles away from the field.

Jones wanted to draft Moss. Whether or not Irvin was going to play forever wasn't important because the Cowboys believed they had another run in them with Troy Aikman, Emmitt Smith, and Irvin. Adding Moss just enhanced the product.

But people inside the organization were concerned. New coach Gailey wasn't a big fan of Moss. Wide receivers coach Dwain Painter was against drafting him as well.

The Cowboys had the No. 8 overall pick in the 1998 NFL Draft. There were needs along the defensive and offensive lines, and upgrading those two positions were important. Yet, bypassing Moss was something the Cowboys couldn't do.

Jones wanted to make sure his franchise made the right decisions on and off the field. Off the field, there were major concerns with the arrests of Irvin and Williams. The reputation of the Cowboys was harsh. In 1997 Jones hired Calvin Hill to enhance its player development program. Hill had created a similar program with the Cleveland Browns when that franchise was going through drug issues on its football team. Hill was drafted in the second round by the Cowboys in 1969. He played six seasons before leaving for the World Football League. The respect for Hill's post-NFL career was tremendous. He helped shape a drug program for the Browns, and Jones was seeking similar programs with his organization. This was a franchise trying to get a hold of troubled souls. Hill, who is the father of Naismith Memorial Hall of

Famer Grant Hill, came in with counselors ready to become an ear for players.

The Cowboys were so interested in Moss that Sanders was recruited to speak with him. Jones wanted as many opinions as possible regarding the talented wide receiver. Moss went to Sanders' house to chat. "The love that I received and the conversations that I had for those 48 hours had me believing that I was going to be a Dallas Cowboy up until draft day," Moss said in an ESPN interview in 2010.

A few weeks before the NFL draft, the Cowboys conducted meetings with Jerry Jones, Stephen Jones, director of pro and college scouting Larry Lacewell, the coaches, and, of course, the scouts. Every meeting was videotaped. Several years prior, a scout was caught trying to change a grade on a prospective player by going into one of the many binders the Cowboys have on prospects. So Jones elected to have the conversations recorded so that no scout, coach, or team executive could have revisionist history. The videotapes were logged with the date and time of the conversation, so anybody could watch them again.

Jones kept seeking more information on Moss. With the NFL draft nearly a week away, Lacewell told pro scout Glenn Smith to visit Marshall. Smith wouldn't invest time into draft picks. Instead, his job was to evaluate NFL players during the season.

This was different.

Smith had a relationship with some of the assistant coaches at Marshall, so his objective was to get a true opinion of Moss from the people who knew him. The Cowboys had the police reports on the fight in high school and college. There was nothing in those reports that gave them insight into the type of person and player Moss was. This was a 21-year-old man they were thinking of drafting high in the first round. If Moss was going to play in Dallas despite his troubled background, Jones wanted every question answered and every stone unturned.

Smith stayed in Charleston, West Virginia, before driving to Huntington, West Virginia. Smith's report was detailed and also honest. "He could have played in the NBA," Smith said of Moss' athletic ability.

On the failed drug test at Florida State, Smith said, "A half a joint, a damn roach. They throw him out."

On his issues with playing college football in-state: "Had to come back hat in hand. There were no issues with him at Marshall."

Smith spent time with Moss and his attorney Dante DiTrapano. "He was a quiet kid, a little introverted," Smith said of Moss. "Nice kid. Well-spoken. Nothing I could get on that kid other than he was from backwoods America like it or not."

In the week leading to the draft, Moss had a strong belief he was going to play for the Cowboys. Here was a scout basically staying near him to get every last piece of information on him.

The 1998 NFL Draft had two quarterbacks—Peyton Manning and Ryan Leaf—at the top of draft boards. The Indianapolis Colts had the No. 1 pick, so the only issue was which quarterback they valued the most. Manning had the appearance he was the most polished of the two, but Leaf's strong arm was difficult to bypass. There were numerous defensive players regarded very high, which included Ellis, along with several other defensive ends. Cornerback Charles Woodson was the best defensive back in the draft and he was slated as a top 10 pick. Offensive linemen Kyle Turley and Tra Thomas were expected to go in the top 15 along with running back Curtis Enis and Moss.

One of the biggest question marks evolved around Moss and whether he was worth taking a risk on. The St. Louis Rams had taken Moss off their draft board and so had the Patriots.

With the draft being held in New York, Moss and Ellis took the same approach to watching it. Moss was in Charleston, watching the draft with his mother and friends. Ellis stayed at a hotel in Chapel Hill.

The night before the draft, Greg and Tangie Ellis had a big meal. "People probably expected us to go to some real big fancy place," Greg Ellis said. "But, man, we just ended up going to the Waffle House, man. But again I don't know if I'm going to get drafted or not. I mean, well, I said I knew it, but I was like: is it going to be or not? It's going to be the next day. So that approach served us very well."

One player had the expectation he would go high, while the other wasn't so sure despite everything he had been told. "I just really took everything [the scouts] said with a grain of salt," Ellis said. "Now my agent [Butch Williams] kept me abreast who it was looking like and who he was hearing from. He did his job like he was supposed to do it."

Ellis recalled former Cowboys team executive Gil Brandt reaching out to him and his head coach at North Carolina, Mack Brown, in the weeks leading up to the draft. "Gil and Mack Brown are real close," Ellis said. "They developed an excellent relationship. Gil called me and told me, 'Greg, Dallas is going to draft you.' I wasn't 100 percent convinced."

Ellis' draft party in Chapel Hill didn't have numerous television cameras waiting inside the hotel suite. Moss' did. There was an ESPN reporter, Linda Cohn, doing live reports inside the home where Moss was holding his draft party. The conversations were vivid about Moss. Andrea Kremer, another ESPN reporter, said she received a physiological report on Moss from an NFL team that wasn't favorable. Cohn also received one, but it was positive. Discussions about Moss from NFL teams were mixed. The television coverage was harsh, particularly from anonymous scouts questioning Moss' character.

The draft unfolded predictably with Manning going No. 1 to the Colts and Leaf No. 2 to the San Diego Chargers. Wadsworth went No. 3 overall to the Arizona Cardinals.

Then the fun began.

In Irving the Cowboys gathered in their war room to speak about Moss and whether he should be the pick at No. 8 if he was available. Jerry Jones, Lacewell, and Gailey sat in front of the room, wearing white shirts and ties. Phones were placed in front of Jones in case he wanted to make a trade with another team. But this wasn't about a trade. This was about a selection.

Jones and Lacewell were good on Moss. So was Smith, who continued to stay in West Virginia, watching the draft from his hotel room. Gailey and Dwain Painter were against it.

Veteran scout Jim Garrett wasn't afraid to speak up. NFL teams desire scouts to speak up when it comes to draft prospects. An NFL coach, whether he's the head coach or position coach, could miss the big picture with a player. Scouts sometimes can better envision what a prospective draft pick could do.

Garrett saw the next Michael Irvin in Randy Moss. He knew about the troubled background. But Garrett knew ballplayers and he loved what Moss could bring to the Cowboys offense. "Men, this is not the Boy Scouts we're dealing with," Garrett told people in the war room. "This is pro football. Draft him."

It wasn't a calm Garrett who was speaking on Moss. Garrett was standing up and talking about Moss.

The Cowboys had so many problems away from the field, it seemed unfair to Gailey, a rookie head coach, to not only deal with Irvin and the rest of a veteran-laden club, but to also bring Moss in with his own baggage. Yet, Garrett's plea was strong. "He's legendary for having said that," Jones told ESPN. "And he said it like he was Billy Graham."

"This guy is unbelievable, a freak," Smith told the war room by home. "It came down to the very last second. I was on the phone with them screaming, 'Pull the trigger.'"

Back in Chapel Hill, Williams' cellphone rang. Rumors were flying that the Cowboys were going to trade up with the Chicago Bears to go from No. 8 to No. 5. Williams and Ellis were trying to figure out what was happening. Maybe Ellis would become the third defensive player taken off the board. When the Bears selected Enis at No. 5, it meant everything was set up for something else. St. Louis at No. 6 took Wistrom. "The phone rang again, and it was the Cowboys saying, 'Okay, Greg we're going to draft you,'" Ellis said. "And I'm thinking like, *Okay sure. I believe that when I see it.*"

Moss sat in West Virginia, and Ellis sat in North Carolina. Both men waited. "Yeah, when Paul Tagliabue called my name, they can't change them out. It's official. It is happening," Ellis said. "And that was it, man."

The Cowboys couldn't pick Moss. Instead, they selected Ellis with the No. 8 overall pick, leaving Moss on the draft board and a head coach relieved. "So now I'm depressed," Moss said. "I'm hurt."

The Cowboys were one of 19 teams to bypass Moss. Moss went No. 21 to Minnesota.

Smith then headed home. He checked out of his hotel in Charleston and drove to Lexington, Kentucky, to catch a flight back to Dallas.

The flight was at 8:00 AM, and as he boarded the plane, he noticed some horseracing jockeys on his flight. Smith felt down about not getting Moss but also understood why the Cowboys selected Ellis, a safer pick for a franchise wanting to upgrade their defensive line.

It didn't make Smith feel better. He sat in the back of the plane next to a jockey and had a present for him. He gave the jockey a Cowboys jersey with the No. 1 on the front. It was meant for Moss.

RANDY MOSS NEVER forgot what the Dallas Cowboys did or didn't do to him. Moss isn't the first player the Cowboys told they were going to draft. Before the 2016 NFL Draft, cornerback Jalen Ramsey said the Cowboys told him he was going to get drafted, but Dallas picked running back Ezekiel Elliott instead.

Moss took Dallas not selecting him as a slight. A major one. In his rookie season, Minnesota faced Dallas at Texas Stadium on November 26, 1998. Moss went off, catching three passes for 163 yards with three touchdowns. In another Thanksgiving Day game in 2000, Moss caught seven passes for 144 yards with two touchdowns. In seven career games, Moss had 35 catches for 662 yards with 10 touchdowns against the Cowboys. Moss had double-digit touchdown receptions against just five teams, and one of them was Dallas. Moss never, ever, ever, forgot. Or even forgave Dallas.

Jerry Jones said it was a regret, but at that time, Moss' off-the-field issues scared Dallas. Michael Irvin said years after that draft that his own issues might have influenced what the Cowboys decided with Moss.

So what did the Cowboys miss in Moss? A six-time Pro Bowler elected to the All-Decade team in 2000, he led the NFL in touchdown receptions five times. And yes, he was elected to the Pro Football Hall of Fame.

His resume just makes Ellis look like a failure. Ellis' career shouldn't be considered that despite being compared to Moss. Ellis played 12 years in the NFL and was named the NFL's Comeback Player of the Year in 2007 while recording 12-and-a-half sacks. Ellis was one of the leaders and mentors to younger linebackers such as DeMarcus Ware.

6

MARCUS SPEARS AND DEMARCUS WARE

JERRY JONES IS a man of risk. He risked it all financially to buy the Dallas Cowboys in 1989. His first significant hire was a college coach and his former college teammate, Jimmy Johnson, as his head coach. It drew a negative reaction from the fanbase and media. Jones even made financial decisions that challenged the traditional way the NFL operates.

The Cowboys owner was proven right in the 1990s. His franchise won three Super Bowl titles in four seasons. However, there were questions about who was responsible for the Super Bowl titles: Johnson or Jones. The current Cowboys owner and general manager, Jones, believed he was the glue for the success. Years later, Jones would admit the titles wouldn't have come without Johnson. The pair's relationship was fractured at one time, but over the years, they grew to respect each other. Johnson was not only inducted into the Pro Football Hall of Fame, but one day

Jones also hopes to put the former coach into the Cowboys' Ring of Honor. Of course, Jones is in the Pro Football Hall of Fame, too. It seems fitting that one of the more valued franchises in sports would have two people, who reshaped the image, be inducted into Canton, Ohio.

Ego damaged the relationship. Maybe the hard-firing Johnson can only be employed for a short period of time before his voice gets ignored. But the Cowboys players felt differently. They wanted Johnson long term. The anger expressed by his departure was symbolized when Michael Irvin threw a plastic trash can at reporters from inside the locker room on the day Johnson's removal became complete.

Johnson was a man who didn't stay employed long. He lasted five years as the head coach of Oklahoma State. Five more at the University of Miami. Five with the Cowboys. He finally cashed checks from the Miami Dolphins for four seasons. Johnson's longest place of employment was at FOX Sports. He started there in 2000 after leaving the Dolphins and he remains with the network to this day. And even that is limited. He gets to the FOX Sports studios for Sunday games in Los Angeles and quickly leaves for his home in Florida. It's like he's got one foot out the door at all times.

Replacing Johnson was difficult on the surface. For Jones, though, it was pretty easy. He hired Barry Switzer, another college coach, and while Switzer won a Super Bowl title—the third in the Jones ownership tenure—there was a different belief around the Cowboys. Switzer wasn't a hard-driving coach like Johnson was, and that irked Troy Aikman. The Cowboys had gotten soft.

Jones had positive thoughts that his team was still good. Jones believed the blueprint he devised with Johnson was good.

The Cowboys, in Jones' eyes, were thriving. The Cowboys, in Jones' eyes, were still relevant. Most importantly, Jones never wavered in his thinking: the Cowboys were still Super Bowl contenders.

After Jones fired Johnson, he went through three more coaching changes: Switzer, Chan Gailey, and finally Dave Campo. In later years, Jones said he regretted firing Gailey after two seasons. Gailey said the roster that produced three Super Bowls was old. He wanted to move on, but Jones waited. Jones believed in the stars of his team, mainly the triplets of quarterback Aikman, running back Emmitt Smith, and wide receiver Irvin. Jones believed in his players. He believed in them too much. He didn't realize until it was too late when it was time to let go.

So Jones moved on from Gailey and asked Campo to take over. It was a surprise hire, but considering Jones' first head coach, Johnson, why would it be a surprise? Campo was a secondary coach/defensive coordinator who didn't get much help. Some scouts believed they failed Campo in the NFL draft. When the narrative of Jones running the draft without strong input from scouts or ignoring scouts surfaced, it was hard to dismiss. The Cowboys failed to draft for Campo in a way that led to success. There were three consecutive 5–11 seasons.

Campo looked overmatched as a head coach. The Cowboys franchise was floundering.

It looked like a repeat of what Tom Landry went through in the late 1980s. It's what prompted the franchise to lose money and eventually get sold to Jones. This time, the franchise wasn't getting sold. Dallas wasn't even losing money. Jones turned the franchise into a winning business off the field. His marketing of the franchise was a master's class on how to turn a losing business into a successful enterprise. On the field, the franchise was stale. It was struggling to find success.

Jones' power as general manager wasn't waning, but he needed to rebuild. He needed to find someone to work with him. It was hard to do that. Jones doesn't do easy. Jones doesn't do quick. He does what's right for his franchise. What he thinks is right.

During the 2002 season, Jones believed a new voice was needed. On December 18, 2002, Jones flew from Dallas to Teterboro Airport, a private airport in New Jersey nearly 12 miles from the Lincoln Tunnel that leads into New York City. Jones was holding an unofficial meeting with the retired Bill Parcells. Jones landed, and Parcells talked to Jones for five hours on the plane while it was on the ground.

When Parcells left the meeting, it gave Jones a hint he had his next head coach. It appeared Parcells was coming out of retirement.

Campo, meanwhile, was fighting through another bad season with his job on the edge of a cliff. Jones wasn't going to save Campo. Jones respected Campo, but he loved and respected the Cowboys more. Jones was going to push Campo off the cliff.

It was Jones' job to fix this franchise again. It was something he accomplished when he purchased the franchise in 1989. Then he fired Landry. There was no doubt this was the right thing to do in his mind at the time. The optics were bad, but it didn't matter. Landry had to go. But that was a long time ago.

Moving forward, Jones hired Parcells in 2003. Parcells in some ways was like Johnson.

He was a short-timer. His hard-driving ways wore on players, his coaches, and even owners. But they loved Parcells. In 19 years as a head coach, Parcells' tenuous career could be described as hotel stays. He ran the New York Giants for eight seasons. Four with the New England Patriots and three with the New York Jets. Four in Dallas. Parcells' intensity took a toll on him, too. Health was ignored. Wins were embraced.

The perception of Parcells is that he was a control freak. All Parcells waned to do is fix a franchise. As he famously said while his coaching tenure ended in New England following the 1996 season: "It's just like a friend of mine told me. If they want you to cook the dinner, at least they ought to let you shop for some of the groceries."

Jones was a man who wanted control, too. Would he let Parcells shop? Could these two work together? It was answered at the news conference introducing Parcells to Cowboys Nation. "I don't want to get into details about my change of philosophy," Jones said. "I frankly think Bill says a lot about how much this organization is willing to win…I've made a lot of mistakes. You know I have. I am not going to be careless with this relationship."

This was Parcells' fourth head coaching gig. At that time, it appeared his last shot at a third ring. He was 61 when he became the head coach. Parcells had said numerous times he didn't coach for the money. He coached because this life was a drug to him. He used the word narcotic. Older coaches, regardless of how many titles you have—and Parcells had two Super Bowl titles and three appearances on his resume—know at a certain point that time runs out. It's the business of the NFL. "I know the window of opportunity was definitely closing on me," he said. "This opportunity, this situation has a nice appeal to me."

Parcells wanted to buy the groceries. Or at least have a say in what was getting picked up at the market. That meant players. Parcells had a type for his team. He wanted tough players who could play multiple positions for years. If one team didn't believe in a particular player, Parcells saw something else. He saw a role. It could be 15 to 20 snaps a game. It could be just on third down. It could be only special teams. It wasn't a special formula. It was Parcells' way of getting things accomplished.

Jones also had a way with things. There would be Jones letting Parcells have his way. There was also Parcells letting Jones have his way. Compromise is a special word in sports, particularly when it comes to head coach and owner or head coach and general manager. In the Cowboys' case, this was Parcells and Jones. Head coach and owner/general manager. Jones didn't believe in middle men. He believed that if you wanted something done, just contact him. It was the best way.

Jones' Super Bowl titles gave him the bullet points on his resume that he was headed in the proper direction. Parcells' own bullet points allowed him to have a loud voice. Two strong-minded, well-informed men were trying to push the Cowboys back to Super Bowl berths. When the 2005 NFL Draft approached, Parcells was in his third season and sensing a change with his team. He felt it couldn't take the next step without a strong draft. While impatient at times, Jones understood the patience in Parcells. Yet, both men knew in Year Three, it was time to see more wins than losses. Parcells wasn't near the cliff that Campo was in that 2002 season, but cracks were showing. Parcells wanted no part of cracks. He sought victories. He sought positive progress. "This thing has always been about winning for us," said Stephen Jones, Jones' son and right-hand man.

The Cowboys had obtained an extra first-round pick after trading with the Buffalo Bills so that Buffalo could draft first-rounder J.P. Losman, a quarterback who didn't pan out, in 2004.

Dallas acquired the Bills' 2005 first-round selection in addition to second- and fifth-round picks. So when the 2005 NFL Draft occurred, the Cowboys would have two first-round selections.

Before reaching the 2005 season, the Cowboys defense was in shambles. It allowed 330 yards per game and 25.3 points per game. It's the major reason why Dallas finished 6–10. In probably the lowest point of that 2004 season, the Cowboys were beaten 26–3 at the Cincinnati Bengals. "This is the only team I can ever remember having that I can't get to respond in the right way, no matter how hard I try," Parcells said. "I feel like I'm having trouble with elementary things. Either I'm not communicating right, or they're not paying enough attention. One of the two. And I assume it's me."

Parcells was dealing with a defensive alignment change. Parcells was a 3-4 defensive coach, which meant three defensive linemen anchored by a nose tackle who could muck up the middle of the line of scrimmage. Parcells wanted inside linebackers to shed blockers and make tackles and outside pass rushers to cause problems off the edge. It was a simple formula but one that desired the right type of players.

Parcells tinkered with a 3-4 and a 4-3 defensive alignment in the first two seasons on the job. He was forced to keep the 4-3 because of the type of personnel he inherited when he was hired in 2003. When the 2004 season ended, it was time for a complete change. Parcells sought a full commitment to the 3-4. He wasn't opposed to a 4-3 because when the Cowboys added an extra defensive back it meant four down linemen were on the field. With NFL teams focusing on passing with an increased frequency, adding four cornerbacks on the field became prevalent in addition to four down linemen.

Parcells explained to Jones what was needed for his defense. Parcells was also dealing with a quarterback issue, going from rookies (Quincy Carter) and former baseball players (Chad Hutchinson and Drew Henson) to veterans. Parcells knew defense was the best way to fix the Cowboys. So when the 2005 NFL Draft approached, there were two players high on his list: DeMarcus Ware and Marcus Spears.

Both players filled a need. Ware was a defensive end, and Spears could play defensive tackle and defensive end. Whether or not those players would be available when the draft approached was an issue. Dallas had picks No. 11 and No. 20 overall in the first round. With any draft an unpredictable force, it's hard to figure out who is available to select. But there was one player who Parcells loved: Spears.

Marcus Spears was an outstanding athlete in high school. He was a two-sport star at Southern Lab School in Baton Rouge, Louisiana. Basketball and football were his best sports.

Football is where he got the attention. He was the No. 1 rated tight end prospect by SuperPrep, a high school recruiting service. That same service ranked Spears as No. 3 overall in the country.

Spears was an athletically gifted tight end who was difficult to contain. He was first-team All-State not just on offense. In 2001 he was a first-team player on defense and offense. He was the first player in Louisiana to get both honors since 1991. The athletic ability in basketball, where he averaged 23.7 points and 15 rebounds per game, translated to the football field as well.

In Spears' senior season, he caught 25 passes for 449 yards and three touchdowns. He also rushed for 245 yards and six touchdowns. The then-6'4" and 270-pound tight end also threw two touchdown passes. Add it up, and Spears had 11 touchdowns.

He was a Class 1A All-State player. Spears' high school, Southern Lab, lost in the state championship game. It won a state title in basketball. When he finished high school, Spears was a two-time MVP of the state title game. He was everything you wanted in a player.

When National Signing Day occurred on February 7, 2001, LSU had picked the top six players in the state. It had among the best recruiting classes in the country. It could thank coach Nick Saban. "Recruiting is not an exact science, and you probably know that," Saban told *The Shreveport Times*. "Football is different from any other sport. It is almost like picking puppy dogs. When you take the pick of the litter, it will always take two or three years to know what that dog is supposed to be like. It is the same in football because I think there is a very important maturity process at this time in a player's life relative to how they develop from the time we recruit them in high school to the time they become productive college football players."

Like Parcells, Saban had a vision for Spears. He wanted Spears to switch positions. Spears was an excellent tight end in high school, but Saban felt the young player could have an impact on defense. It wasn't a glamour spot. It was a position where Spears could excel not only in college, but also in the NFL. Spears needed to commit to it. He needed to believe in Saban. He believed in Saban enough to play for him out of high school. While at LSU the bond between the men grew. Spears would go fishing at Saban's house as if he owned the land. Now he needed to believe in him even more.

Spears was going to morph into a defensive end/tackle. In that freshman season, Spears participated at three positions: tight end, fullback, and defensive end. Spears was so good at

Marcus Spears celebrates after stopping the Buffalo Bills on a fourth-and-1 play during a game at Ralph Wilson Stadium in October of 2007.

tight end he was named to the freshman All-SEC team. In 2002 Spears moved to the defensive side full time, making 12 starts along the line. As a junior Spears excelled, becoming a first-team All-SEC selection. Spears thought about turning pro after that junior season. It was hard to bypass the NFL, considering the money that was in front of him. He was considered a first-round selection from some NFL scouts, but the negative was the weight. If he was going to play as a defensive lineman in the NFL, he needed to bulk up.

Height wasn't an issue. At 6'4" everything seemed right for Spears. But the 298 pounds he maintained needed changing. It wasn't a good 298 pounds. Spears came into nearly every training camp out of shape. So that senior season, Spears transformed to add muscle while keeping his quickness. In his senior season, Spears was a first-team All-American and had nine sacks, 17 tackles for loss, and 21 quarterback hurries. It was the fourth most tackles for loss in a single season in school history.

As LSU prepared for the national title game that season, agents swarmed him. There was no going back for Spears. He knew it was time to turn professional. The only issue for Spears was how quickly would he get drafted.

DEMARCUS WARE'S HEAD was spinning. At Auburn High School, Ware started playing football in his junior year. At 6'3" and 196 pounds, he was built more like a basketball player. In high school he played baseball but rarely took an at-bat. He excelled at patrolling the outfield.

Yet, playing football was his best sport. But you would never know it by the amount of schools that recruited Ware. When he finished his two seasons at Auburn High, Ware had just one scholarship offer: Troy University.

Ware was hopeful to get a scholarship from Alabama, Auburn, or somewhere else. In high school while working the concessions stands of Auburn's Jordan-Hare Stadium, he wondered why the big college in his hometown didn't look at him seriously.

Going into his senior season, Ware was among the players named as "Best of the Rest" in the *Montgomery Advertiser* in 2000. He didn't have the name recognition in the media or with the big-named colleges. When his senior season ended, he had 40 solo tackles and seven sacks, but he still had no big time offers other than Troy.

It was probably fitting that Ware and Troy would become a partnership. Troy was moving to the Football Bowl Subdivision for the 2001 season. For several years Troy was a Division I AA program and now it was moving to Division I to play with the big boys. So Troy and Ware had a chance to show everyone their talents.

After three seasons at Troy, Ware was no longer the best of the rest. NFL teams knew he was one of the best. Ware finished his career as the school's all-time leader in tackles for loss (55.5) to go with his 27.5 sacks. As a sophomore during the 2002 season, the starting defensive end combined with Osi Umenyiora for 25 sacks and 40 tackles for loss. Ware alone had nine sacks to rank 15th in the nation. In 2003 Ware led the team with 32 quarterback hurries, five forced fumbles, and two fumble recoveries. The next season Ware was named Sun Belt Conference Defensive Player of the Year, and Troy played in a Division I bowl game for the first time. Ware had 53 tackles and a conference-leading 10.5 sacks. The transformation for Troy and Ware was complete. The school was considered a legit Division I program with the ability to compete for conference titles and bowl games. Ware had gone from a man who had one scholarship offer to numerous NFL teams seeking his services.

The only problem for Ware and Marcus Spears was weight. Spears was too heavy. Ware was too light. Spears could play defensive end and defensive tackle. If an NFL team sought Spears to play off the edge in a 3-4 alignment, he needed to be roughly 300 pounds. If Ware was to play defensive end in the NFL, then it was necessary to get a little heavier. If Ware was to play outside linebacker in a 3-4 scheme, then being lighter to get after the quarterback was needed. NFL teams projected him at defensive end. "That's where I've played in the last four years," Ware told the *Star-Telegram*. "I've played against some 300, 340-pound tackles in college and I know I would have to in the NFL. But if I critique myself a lot, watch the film, watch what they do, watch what I do, and always try to get better, I think I can compete. All I need is a chance."

Ware knew he needed a strong draft process to increase his stock. The odds were against him because he played in what NFL scouts believed was a small school. And Ware was light, roughly 250 pounds. His projection was a second- or third-round selection. Sensing this, Ware took charge of his draft process. It started in the Senior Bowl in Mobile, Alabama, one of the first games where draft prospects can showcase their skills. Ware displayed speed off the edge, something NFL coaches wanted to see. He also had power. His big hands and long arms allowed him to push off offensive tackles, and once past the men assigned to block him, his quickness was a mismatch for running backs who were the last line of defense for a quarterback.

After the Senior Bowl, which saw his stock rise, he went to the NFL Scouting Combine in Indianapolis. Ware tore up the Combine. He was hand timed in the 40-yard dash at 4.56 seconds, an amazing speed for a linebacker that was measured at 251 pounds. He bench pressed 225 pounds 27 times. He displayed a vertical leap of 38½ inches. His time in the three-cone drill, which measures the quickness and flexibility of a pass rusher, was seven seconds. Ware went from small-school prospect with an unknown draft selection to a possible first-round pick. He emerged as one of the top pass rushers in the NFL draft.

In most mock drafts, the top two pass rushers were Maryland's Shawne Merriman and Ware. But Ware needed one more event: his Pro Day on his college campus. It was raining, and while scouts said he could run inside, Ware wanted to prove something to them. "I told myself, *Football is played in the rain, snow, heat, etc.*," he said. "*You need to show these scouts that it doesn't matter.* I made them follow me outside in the rain and I ran."

Ware's Pro Day 40 time was hand timed at 4.45. Did he get faster? Sure. All the scouts take the slowest time and officially use it for their personal records for their respective teams: Ware's Pro Day time was 4.53. Now there was no doubt regarding Ware's ability to become a first-round pick. "I knew my mom had bills to pay," Ware said.

He knew running in the rain was a questionable decision. So much could go wrong. He could slip and get injured. The slick track might cause a slower time, raising doubts about his true abilities. Instead he showed his perseverance. Ware picked up 14 pounds from the end of his senior season at Troy to the Pro Day. If you wanted Ware to play outside linebacker, he could do that.

If you wanted Ware to play defensive end, sure, he could play that, too. It was a matter of figuring out what to do with him.

So Ware, a man who dreamed of playing for Auburn, a man who was engaged to be married, a man who wanted to take care of family, particularly his mom, gambled on that Pro Day in Troy, Alabama. Everything worked out for him. "I had a choice," he said. "But I wasn't giving [the scouts] a choice of thinking if I'm serious and wanted it or not."

Ware wanted it. All that was left was finding a team that wanted him in the first round as a pass rusher. He had improved his stock. "I think so," Ware said at the Combine. "I've tried to show I can compete with everybody. I played hard and when I get the opportunity I want to show the coaches and everybody in the NFL I can do it."

Spears' draft process was different than Ware's. Spears came from the big-time school, LSU, with a big-time coach, Nick Saban, and the accolades. He participated in the Senior Bowl and impressed scouts with his ability to play end and defensive tackle. He was slated to play a three-technique position, where the defensive tackle is shaded over the outside shoulder of the guard, near the tackle. Spears' weight of 300-plus pounds allowed him to get pressure up the middle. The hardest part was evaluating Spears' ability to push the pocket against bigger men.

At the Senior Bowl, Tampa Bay Buccaneers defensive coordinator Monte Kiffin raved about Spears to *The Town Talk*, a newspaper in Alexandria, Louisiana. "Very, very smart, loves football," Kiffin said. "He comes to work every day. I really like him. He's bigger than Booger [McFarland] who's more of a nose tackle, three-technique guy. This guy's a big end. He's going to be a good player. He's going to be in the league a long time."

DeMarcus Ware gets ready to rush the passer in 2006, a year in which he had 11.5 sacks for Bill Parcells' revamped defense.

McFarland was from Winnsboro, Louisiana, and also played at LSU. He was the 15th overall pick by Tampa Bay in 1999. So Kiffin already had his inside defensive tackle and he was projecting Spears for end. Then again, did it matter where you played Spears? He was a difficult player to block. "Everybody's talking about Marcus Spears," Tampa Bay coach Jon Gruden said during the Senior Bowl. "He's a very good football player."

Spears did his part in the Senior Bowl. But after the Senior Bowl, Spears injured his knee while preparing for the Combine. In February of 2005, Spears underwent surgery on his right knee. It was described as minor, but Spears required surgery for a partially torn meniscus. Any injury pushes a player's stock down. It could make a first-round pick a second- or third-round selection. NFL teams invest money, draft capital, and time on prospects, and the healthier the better.

The game tape and the practice work during the seasons are where the best evaluations come from. The college bowl games, All-Star Games such as the Senior Bowl and East-West Shrine Game, Combine, and Pro Days are just part of the process. "Most teams will tell you at best this piece of the puzzle should be about 20 percent," former Atlanta Falcons general manager Rich McKay said. "Eighty percent, and in some cases maybe more, is based on body of work. It's based on the way the guy has played and what he put on tape. Now, when we get to the level of competition, that changes a little bit. You get the guy who's played for a small college or played against lesser competition, then you know what? This piece will start to mean a little bit more because you'll have to confirm times, speeds, and look at athleticism that—because of that level of competition—you couldn't judge."

Spears wasn't concerned about his stock dropping, though the injury raised questions about his health. Did weight contribute to the knee issue? Was the knee problem just the price of playing football? Most players get some sort of procedure at some point of their careers, whether it's in college or the pros.

Spears didn't work out at the Combine. He just interviewed with NFL teams. But the questions from the media and NFL teams about his health didn't stop. "I got my knee scoped two weeks ago, and it's coming along fine," he said. "I've been cleared by doctors to do a little bit, but I'm just going to hold off until my Pro Day."

The Pro Day was a possibility for him to showcase himself one last time. The other question Spears faced was whether he could play in either a 4-3 or 3-4 scheme. "The 3-4 questions have come up a lot through this whole process," Spears said. "I'm able—and I'm willing—to play in either scheme. Each has their advantages. Whatever coach I have, it will be whatever he likes, but I'll be able to do both."

Spears said all the right things. There was no question in his mind if he could play defensive end or defensive tackle. "Wouldn't mind it at all," he said. "I played a little bit of tackle, and it's pretty much the same thing, just a lot more cloudy in there."

While Spears was set, Bill Parcells was worried. That's what he does. It doesn't matter if it's about a racehorse he owns or a player he wants drafted. He worries. He can drive you crazy, but that's what most NFL coaches do. They worry.

When the 2004 season ended, the Dallas Cowboys' 4-3 front was on the way out. Defensive ends Marcellus Wiley and Greg Ellis combined for 12 sacks. La'Roi Glover and Jason Ferguson, the two defensive tackles, were still valued members to rotate inside. Among the veterans, Wiley wasn't returning for the 2005 season. So that meant Glover, Ferguson, and Ellis were part of the 3–4 scheme change.

Parcells loved veterans. He valued them more than rookies because of their experience. But if a rookie player displayed talent, then he was getting playing time. He thought Spears could be that kind of player and that Spears could begin the process of moving from a 4-3 alignment to a 3-4 alignment. He wanted Spears to man the edge as the big defensive end.

Parcells also desired Ware. In the move to 3-4, Parcells sought an outside pass rusher with speed and power. During the draft process, NFL teams are allowed 20 visits. The players visit the team facilities and get a tour of their potential future home. It also allows coaches, front-office personnel, and scouts to interview a player in a relaxed environment. The Cowboys also have what they call "Dallas Day." It's a time where potential draft prospects can visit the facility because they have area ties. Spears was from Louisiana, and Ware was from Alabama. So neither player was on either list. Ware had a visit that was scheduled, but it got canceled.

There was one player who did visit the Cowboys' complex in Irving, Texas: Merriman.

The Maryland product was considered one of the top pass rushers in the draft. During his visit to the Cowboys' Valley Ranch complex, he described a scene that convinced him about his future: "We're all in the locker room. Jerry Jones and Bill Parcells sent somebody to get me, just me," Merriman recalled on the podcast called *Catchin' Fades with Aqib Talib*. "They say, 'Hey we've got the No. 11 pick. We don't think you're going to be here. We think you'll go somewhere in the top five. But if you're there, we're going to draft you.'"

Merriman said he felt Dallas was in his plans. Ware has said Parcells wanted Merriman.

It worried Ware about whether the Cowboys wanted him or not. Spears wasn't sure what was going on. Yet, Parcells knew. Or he thought he knew.

As the draft grew closer, he became more and more agitated. The Cowboys had the No. 11 and No. 20 overall selections. There were several players linked to the Cowboys in the 2005 draft outside of Merriman, Ware, and Spears. Derrick Johnson, a linebacker from the University of Texas, was a possibility. But that was more media talk than what the Cowboys thought inside their facility in Irving, Texas. The Cowboys had a fondness for Wisconsin pass rusher Erasmus James. Like Spears, he had his own health issues. James' was more serious due to a hip injury.

There was also a question if James could even play in a 3-4 scheme. "I'd be very good in a 3-4," James said at the Combine. "I can be good against the run. I got great hip extension, and this past year I've proven to the scouts that I can stop the run. I feel very comfortable."

Most if not all NFL draft evaluators believe the process is unpredictable. That's why teams send out false information to reporters or scouts. It's this cat and mouse game of information. Draft projections from some media members could be formulated from talking to NFL executives. Some draft projections are educated guesses from the media. NFL teams don't know what the team ahead of them is going to do. It's part of a dirty game that's gone on for years. With the Cowboys not inviting Spears and Ware to their team facility, it could mean they were down on them.

But Parcells was nervous in the days leading to the draft. He kept telling Jerry and Stephen Jones he was worried about losing out on Spears, the defensive end he wanted. Cowboys officials told him to relax. Yet he couldn't. The Cowboys scouts believed Spears and Ware could be obtained. But Parcells wanted to trade up to get Spears. With the 11th overall selection, moving into the top 10 to get Spears was a major reach. The night before the draft, Jerry Jones and his son, Stephen, took Parcells out to dinner. It was time to calm him down. Parcells trusted the draft process, but to fix the defense, he wanted to get quality prospects in the first round. And the head coach wanted to make sure he solved some of his problems on the defense.

In 2004 the Cowboys allowed 5,285 yards. For a defensive coach like Parcells, that was unacceptable. Overall, the defense ranked 26th. It allowed a whopping 180 first downs via pass, the most since 1991. What probably bothered Parcells more than anything else was the points allowed: 405. The 400-plus points were the most given up in franchise history. In 1962 the Cowboys, just three years old as a franchise at that point, allowed 402 points. Even the 1989 team that finished 1–15 didn't give up 400-plus points. That sad squad during Jones' first year as the owner gave up 393 points.

So for Parcells the numbers and a lack of emerging talent spoke loudly to him. In his relaxed Arkansas southern drawl, Jerry Jones told him to relax. Spears, the man Parcells loved, was going to be around in the late stages of the first round. Dallas was confident it could get Ware. "There were a lot of edgy feelings and thoughts because we knew the consequences if we didn't get him," Jones said of Spears.

When the dinner ended, Jones thought he calmed Parcells down or at least eased the fears he wouldn't get what he wanted.

When the draft began, Alex Smith went No. 1 overall to the San Francisco 49ers. No surprise there. Then things got exciting. With the draft progressing, Ware thought the Cowboys were out. He figured the San Diego Chargers (No. 12) and Carolina Panthers (No. 14) were his most likely destinations. Based on his visit, Merriman had visions of becoming a Cowboys player. Parcells, of course, worried about losing Spears and kept talking about him in the Cowboys' war room.

Jones, however, remained calm. Jones told Parcells if they couldn't get Spears at No. 20, they'd move up to get him. The better player, based on the draft board, was Ware. "The No. 11 pick came up, and they called DeMarcus," Merriman said. "I'm sitting there like you could hear a pin drop. Everybody's like, 'What happened? What the fuck is going on?'"

Ware sat with family and friends in Auburn, Alabama, watching television in shock. He hugged his agent, fiancee, mother, anybody who was there. Dallas picked Ware at No. 11.

The next step was getting Spears. "I thought I'd be taken at 11," Spears said as he watched the draft.

It was going to be tricky for Spears to fall. Jones made phone calls to move up. No takers. Merriman went No. 12 to San Diego. Thomas Davis was selected by Carolina at No. 14. Johnson went to the Kansas City Chiefs at No. 15. A decision was made in the Cowboys war room. If the team couldn't get Spears and if James was available, they would select James.

But then he went No. 18 to the Minnesota Vikings. The Cowboys waited. "We were anxious, but we made the decision to go for it," Jones said. "You do what you can do and then you live with it if somebody else takes him."

With the St. Louis Rams picking at No. 19, there was a feeling the Rams wouldn't get Spears. But they took offensive lineman Alex Barron.

Then Spears, sitting at home on a couch with a television camera fixed on him, got the call from Jones. Spears went No. 20. Parcells got the two players he wanted most to help with his defense. "We gave up 406 points last year," Parcells said the day the two players were picked. "Thirty one touchdown passes—that is the highest of my career. I know for a fact, if that didn't change, the fortunes of the Cowboys wouldn't change."

Ware admitted to being concerned regarding Dallas' interest in him. "I was hoping they were trying to be low-key and didn't want anybody to know they were interested," he said. "When they canceled my visit, I thought, *Oh my God what's going on? Are they backing off?*"

Not even close. If anything, the Cowboys were preparing to use Ware as either a defensive end or outside linebacker. They knew he was raw in some areas and probably could gain 10 to 15 pounds of muscle. But there was no doubt he was their guy. "I have the speed to get around the corner," Ware said. "And I can run up on the backside and make plays."

Spears' selection was another strong evaluation despite the worrisome nature of whether he was going to be available. He was the last crucial part of the draft process in helping Parcells fix the Cowboys defense. "I can't tell you how many times Bill would wring his hands and say we have to get some pressure," Jones said. "Those two picks give us the pressure we need and can solidify our defensive front with Ellis, Glover, and Ferguson that would be like drawing up our Christmas list."

Spears and Ware were teammates in Dallas for eight seasons. Ware got the fame because he excelled at the glamour position of outside linebacker. He finished a 12-year career with 138-and-a-half sacks to rank ninth all time. Ware was also a nine-time Pro Bowler and a four-time All-Pro. Ware was named to the All-Decade team for the 2000s. Ware is considered one of the great defensive players in franchise history, and many project him to get elected to the Pro Football Hall of Fame. Spears participated at defensive end and defensive tackle. His job was to set the edge, clog the middle if necessary, and do the grunt work. Spears played nine seasons, and his value was as important as Parcells had figured it to be.

7

JOHNNY MANZIEL

THE MEETINGS LASTED all day. It started early, around 8:00 AM when Jerry Jones, the Dallas Cowboys owner and general manager, was using both hats. The NFL draft—the place where NFL teams stock up for the future or the present, depending on where the franchise is currently—was in 24 hours. Jones, wearing his GM hat, wanted to know about the future. His franchise was coming off an 8–8 season in 2013 and needed fixing. Jones' starting quarterback, Tony Romo, was in the first year of a contract extension. In the spring of 2013, Romo signed a six-year, $108-million contract extension with $55 million guaranteed. He finished the season with 31 touchdowns and 10 interceptions in 15 games.

A year later there were questions.

On the surface, Romo was the long-term answer at quarterback for the Cowboys. There was nowhere else to go other than Romo. The contract extension secured not only Romo's future with the franchise, but also was another statement the Cowboys were done searching for a quarterback after years of failures.

But during this May 2014 meeting at the place they call The Ranch, the Cowboys practice facility in Irving, Texas, Jones asked about drafting a quarterback. These meetings are typical before the NFL draft. Everyone has a say if they speak up. It's the first time the scouts, front-office personnel, and ownership can have an open dialogue about talent. During the course of a college football season, these conversations are splintered. Sometimes they occur via text message. Maybe in a phone call. The college scouts are divided into areas of the country. They watch games and practices. They insert information into a computer database for accountability purposes. If a scout places a grade on a player and it's in the computer, there is no taking it back. None. In the old days, a scout could sneak into the war room, where the big board, a listing of all the draft eligible players, is and change a grade. Nobody would know. Nobody.

Now with the computer entries everybody knows.

But 24 hours before the draft, there are no more games and practices to watch or coaches, trainers, parents, teammates to talk with about a prospective player. The visits from prospective draft picks are over with as well. NFL teams are allowed 30 visits to their practice facility from college prospects. So finally, 24 hours before the NFL draft, these final conversations about who to select or who to bypass occur. Sometimes it's to the detriment of a team. If scouts don't speak up, it can lead to poor draft selections instead of meaningful conversations.

The draft process, of course, leads teams in different ways. Coaches can become headstrong about potential draft picks because their vision for that particular player is different from the scouts. The coaches want a say in personnel because they're coaching the talent after all. The problem with coaches having a say is their only legitimate review of a draft prospect isn't live; it's on game tape. Yet, the coaches are the face of the franchise in some cases, and their opinions matter.

The scouts' opinions are valued greatly. These men and women travel across the country to watch games and practices. They talk with coaches, players, family, team trainers, doctors, and teammates. Scouts want to be heard. If ownership is paying scouts to give an honest assessment of a prospect, then let's see what the scout has to say. It doesn't necessarily mean a scout is right about a prospect because the NFL draft is filled with prospects who don't pan out on the field. Some of those same players struggle being a pro away from the field as much as on the field. These are educated guesses, and few can say every prospective player will make it. The projections could mean a player is an instant starter or career backup. Some players don't get drafted and can still have a long career in the NFL. Romo wasn't drafted by the Cowboys. He instead took less money to sign as an undrafted free agent to work with then-coach Bill Parcells and quarterback coach Sean Payton. Romo was lured by the legend of Parcells, a Hall of Fame coach, and Payton, who played quarterback at Eastern Illinois, the same school as Romo.

Ownership, however, can stand in the way of this process. Some owners can't let go of a veteran player so a potential draft pick can move in. The salary cap department has a say because releasing a player causes problems to the cap. Cutting a player can add significant amounts of dead money to a team's bottom line. That's why meetings are held year round about such issues.

Yet the spring is where final decisions are made.

Adding another element to the draft process is free agency that begins in late February/early March. Signing free agents means instant help for a particular position. Some free-agent signings are meant to create competition at various spots. These decisions come with a financial stake. The more you spend on a player, the expectations are increased.

When it comes to the draft, every NFL team has an allocated amount of money to selections. The higher your place in the draft, the more pressure comes with that. Everyone remembers the No. 1 overall pick. Few remember pick No. 183.

What everyone also remembers is the front-office guy, the general manager mainly, who made the right or wrong selections. With the Cowboys that's Jerry Jones.

The great thing about Jones is his ability to shield scouts and personnel people from media questions about draft mistakes. When the media asks questions of Jones regarding draft decisions, he's quick to point out "we" made this call. *We didn't want to do that.* Yet Jones is front and center about the draft, and no decision is made without his final approval. Over the years Jones told reporters it's in the NFL bylaws, allowing owners final say on every decision.

It's a strange passage to have in ownership documents because why wouldn't an owner have final say? It's his or her team. The good owners, the ones who respect the process, listen to the men and women who coach and scout. Jones wants his scouts and personnel people to have a say. He almost demands it. He doesn't make decisions based on just one man. He wants input from everyone. He respects veteran coaches and scouts because years of watching players on college campuses gives them clout. It's probably why there isn't a high turnover in the scouting department around the Cowboys. You could attribute this to Jones' refusal to fire people so he can maintain continuity within a particular department. Jones respects the process people go through in helping him draft players.

As much as Jones loves the meat and potatoes of scouting players, that's the GM side of him. The ownership side of him questions the process. On this early morning of May 7, Jones, acting like the owner of the franchise instead of the general manager, had serious questions. Just based on what the Cowboys paid Romo, why would a general manager care about drafting a quarterback? Romo signed a contract extension and wasn't going anywhere. Sure, Romo was going to be 34 in Week One of the 2014 season, but he was playing for a franchise confident he had years left. So here was Jones asking his coaches, scouts, and front-office staff about Johnny Manziel, the Texas A&M quarterback who just took over college football.

Manziel had one quality Jones liked in his football players: personality. Which also means marketability. Manziel was from Kerrville, Texas, a town of nearly 25,000, where a portion of the Guadalupe River runs through. Manziel had the nickname that any football man would love: Johnny Football. He was from Texas and played at a Texas school, Texas A&M. "Jerry had visions of sugar plums when he was thinking of Johnny Football," said Jones' son, Stephen, in a documentary called *Deep Blue War Stories*. "He can certainly envision what that could mean to the brand. He was certainly a baller and a Heisman Trophy winner."

Manziel's rise to stud quarterback was sudden. In 2012 he was fourth on the depth chart his redshirt freshman season. Manziel was behind Jameill Showers, Matt Joeckel, and Matt

Davis on the depth chart. A June 2012 arrest changed everything. He was forced to apologize to the team after being charged with disorderly conduct and presenting a fake driver's license to police officers in College Station, Texas. The charge was a Class C misdemeanor. The arrest was thought to have doomed Manziel's chance to take the starting job from either Showers or Joeckel. After fall practices Manziel was forced to run laps as punishment for his actions.

Manziel would say later those laps—*gassers* in football parlance—got him in better shape than anybody else on the team. Conditioning? Manziel had it. You could even call it energy. He had that in spades. His ability to move in the pocket allowed him to keep plays alive. Manziel was a dancer on the football field. When the pocket would break down, he was gone. His receivers knew if corners couldn't stick to them and Manziel was moving around, it was playground football. It was fun to watch. Nick Saban, the Alabama head coach, said: "I've been around longer than most, and most of our players can't relate to this, but this guy reminds me of Doug Flutie."

Flutie was a 5'10", 180-pound quarterback with similar skills to Manziel. He could throw on the move and had a strong arm to push the offense downfield. His size didn't help his draft stock with NFL teams, who were used to taller quarterbacks, but the Los Angeles Rams selected him in the 11th round of the 1985 NFL Draft. Flutie was ahead of his time. Since then, quarterbacks shorter than 6'3" and 6'4" had stretches where they took over the league, including Russell Wilson, Kyler Murray, Baker Mayfield, and Michael Vick, among others.

Despite his small stature, Manziel had big aspirations. He just didn't know it yet during that redshirt freshman season. When the

2012 season was over, Manziel became the first freshman to win the Heisman Trophy. He led the SEC in completions (295), completion percentage (68), rushing yards (1,410), and touchdowns (26). He also led the NCAA in total yards with 5,116. Manziel won the Heisman Trophy, collecting 474 first-place votes. It was the most votes since winner Cam Newton's 729 first-place votes in 2010.

Manziel's breakout game came in an upset win against Alabama. It was one of the biggest upsets in college football as Texas A&M, then ranked No. 15 in the Associated Press poll, knocked off No. 1 Alabama. The Aggies were 1–10 all time against a No. 1 ranked opponent until that game.

Manziel was unreal in that game.

He avoided pressure in the pocket with excellent footwork despite holding the ball away from his body, a no-no in the NFL for a signal caller. Manziel did whatever he wanted. During the Alabama game, Manziel lost the ball momentarily when he bumped into an offensive lineman but then snagged it out of the air before throwing touchdown pass. It was magical plays that put Johnny Football on the map. The Aggies took a commanding 20–0 first quarter lead and held off the Crimson Tide's rally. Manziel completed 24-of-31 passes for 253 yards with two touchdowns and 92 rushing yards in a 29–24 road victory.

It not only stunned the Alabama home crowd, but also the national television audience. During the course of the season, Manziel and his teammates were shocked to see his name on ESPN talking about his Heisman Trophy push. For Manziel it was a dream. This was something he would do as a teenager, playing the *NCAA Football* video game on PlayStation or Xbox. You could win the Heisman Trophy four consecutive years playing a video game. Now it was becoming real to Manziel. This was no video game. This was life. This was becoming unreal.

In the Cotton Bowl, a game played in front of Jones' family at Cowboys Stadium in Arlington, Texas, Manziel went wild. Manziel set a Cotton Bowl record with 516 total yards of offense in a 41–13 victory against Oklahoma. He took over Jerry's World, the nickname for Cowboys Stadium, as if he was going to play there soon. Manziel was a new version of Roger Staubach. When Staubach was a quarterback at Navy, he moved around the pocket himself, avoiding pressures to complete passes or get down the field by running the ball. Staubach kept this up in his early years in the NFL. Quarterbacks that move within the pocket keep fans, defenses, and wide receivers on edge. Something magical or terrible seems like it's about to happen.

The great ones have something magical happen. That was Manziel.

Manziel's game against Alabama sealed his place in college football lore.

The next season Manziel was just as good. He finished the season No. 1 in the SEC in pass completions (300), completion percentage (69.9), and was responsible for 46 touchdowns. When his two-year career ended, Manziel was responsible for 93 touchdowns—10th all time in conference history. That final year he threw for 4,114 yards—tops in the conference—but also led the SEC with 13 interceptions.

In his final college game, Manziel led Texas A&M from a 21–3 deficit to defeat Duke 52–48 in the Chick-fil-A Bowl in Atlanta. It ended a season where the Aggies were ranked No. 7 in the preseason AP top 25 poll. An early-season loss to Alabama hurt their chances for national title hopes. For all his magic, Manziel's Aggies went 0–4 against ranked teams in 2013, including losses at LSU and Missouri to end the season. The bowl win against Duke salvaged something of a 9–4 year for the team. For Manziel it meant something else: it was time to go.

After two seasons in College Station, Texas, with a Heisman Trophy in his pocket, he was going pro. No doubt.

And now Jones, the Cowboys owner, was asking about him.

Jones loved how Manziel dazzled college football with his athletic ability and brashness off the field. Nevermind the potential off-the-field problems Manziel presented with his partying lifestyle and his lack of preparation in the classroom. "He knew he could sell a lot of Aggies in Texas and he could sell a lot of jerseys and this and that, but his grade did not reflect that," said an unnamed Cowboys scout on Jones' love for Manziel.

Years later, Manziel would describe his time in College Station simply as a big party. Then life suddenly went out of control with few people to contain it. "That year [2012] is the reason I got in so much trouble down the line because I treated it like a kegger to be honest," Manziel said on the *Ball Don't Lie* podcast. "Every week, Tuesdays and Thursdays, we had a full-blown king's cup, beer olympics at the house drinking Natty Lites, and Old Milwaukee's was on sale for $16.99. That was the best."

NFL teams do tremendous work on prospective draft picks. They send investigators to hometowns and college campuses seeking information. NFL scouts triple-check information about players. Manziel's party lifestyle wasn't hidden. "So if you're watching the tape, you're going, 'well, he's a little bit light [size-wise], Manziel, very immature,'" an unnamed Cowboys scout said.

"And he did not put in the time to be great. Yeah, that's why he failed. So you had that individually in him. But you got [NFL teams] still trying to trade up for it because you think you could fix him. He wasn't a bad kid...Teams think *our culture could get him going* in this and that, so he was in the conversation."

Manziel would party so much that he was hungover some days before heading to practice. Manziel became a rock star on a college campus with dreams of being a bigger star on the NFL stage. His life was going so fast that it was difficult to get a handle on it. Years later, Manziel would blame nobody but himself for his partying. The attention he drew on campus blitzed people around him, including family members, coaches, teammates, and friends. Johnny Football wasn't a caricature but real life.

Jerry Jones is the owner of three Super Bowls rings and is a member of the Pro Football Hall of Fame. Jones changed the way the NFL does business and built one of the best sporting venues in North America in Cowboys Stadium. So in these morning meetings about the NFL draft, Jones, knowing what he's accomplished as a businessman, had visions of Manziel.

The meetings took a different turn for Jones.

Stephen Jones, Jerry Jones' son and the No. 2 man as the executive vice president, was debating with his father. He understood the marketing of Manziel. Here was a Texas-born football player with a brashness that reminded him of his father. Jason Garrett, the Cowboys head coach at the time, also understood the marketing of Manziel. But Garrett and the scouts knew something else: Manziel was a problem. Garrett believed in Romo as the quarterback, but he also played in the 1990s, an era the Cowboys dominated. The Triplets—Troy Aikman, Emmitt Smith, and Michael Irvin—get most of the attention, but the glue to the franchise winning three Super Bowl titles resided with the offensive line.

Garrett had the ear of Stephen Jones regarding rebuilding an offensive line that was put together via free agency and Day Two and Day Three draft picks. In 2011 things began to change. The Cowboys selected USC tackle Tyron Smith with the ninth overall pick in the draft. With the 31st pick of the first round in 2013, Wisconsin center Travis Frederick was snagged. Two starters for the future with tremendous talent. If you want to protect Romo, you better have a good offensive line. Garrett realized this as a backup quarterback. He lived it with Jerry and Stephen Jones. And the Cowboys were again in position to upgrade the offensive line.

The NFL waits for no team to get its act together because, frankly, there is no time.

Garrett spoke to Stephen Jones about Zack Martin, a do-everything offensive lineman at Notre Dame. He was someone who could play guard or tackle for years without worry.

Manziel was a worry. Garrett understood it.

So in this meeting he let Stephen Jones do the talking. He let the scouts do the talking and, of course, he let Will McClay, the vice president of player personnel, talk. Stephen Jones discussed four college prospects with his father: linebacker Anthony Barr from UCLA; Aaron Donald, a defensive tackle from the University of Pittsburgh; Ryan Shazier, the linebacker from Ohio State; and Martin, a guard from Notre Dame. The Cowboys had the No. 16 overall draft pick, and if one of those players was available on Day One of the draft, they would pick one. If the four players the Cowboys expressed interest in were gone, then Manziel was the pick.

No decision was made about who to pick this day. Yet it didn't stop speculation about Manziel getting drafted to the Cowboys with the 16th overall pick in the first round. "I mean, that's a team I grew up rooting for," Manziel said before the draft. "I grew up watching and to be able to know Jerry on a little more personal level now, going to games at his suite or going to Cowboys games at Cowboys Stadium, and to run into him, for me that was something that was really cool. He's a huge figure in the state of Texas. Being from the state of Texas, it was really cool to get a chance to know him more, and the way he treated me has been great. But I would like to go a little bit sooner than that, but it's out of my control, and whatever happens, happens."

The Cowboys did their research on Manziel. They met him at the NFL Scouting Combine, his Pro Day at Texas A&M, and during a visit to the team facility. What the Cowboys did with Manziel was no different than the homework conducted with any other draftable player. Jones had seen Manziel play in person at Cowboys Stadium. The connections between Manziel and Jones were heavy. Jones didn't want to go through years without a QB1 again. When Hall of Famer Troy Aikman retired following the 2000 season, the Cowboys started eight different quarterbacks between 2001 and 2005. Only two quarterbacks, Drew Bledsoe and Quincy Carter, started a full season during this time. Bledsoe was the veteran brought in by Parcells. The need to replace Bledsoe was always present but not forced until Parcells had to insert Romo after six games in the 2006 season. Romo never let go of the starting job, but here was Jones worrying about a flood of quarterbacks being used again should something happen to Romo.

Even though Johnny Manziel looked great—while wearing unusual workout gear—
at his Texas A&M Pro Day, the Dallas Cowboys were wise to pass on him.

How could he not love Manziel? Manziel did everything you could ask during the lead up of the draft. He said all the right things. He acted like a star. It was hard not to love Manziel's personality. His Texas A&M Pro Day was a star-studded event. Former president George H.W. Bush and his wife, Barbara, watched the Pro Day from a golf cart. There were 75 scouts and front-office personnel representing 30 NFL teams watching his Pro Day. Manziel walked into the indoor practice facility wearing camouflage shorts, shoulder pads, and a helmet. Normally quarterbacks don't throw with a helmet, but Manziel did. Manziel wanted to simulate throwing with a helmet and shoulder pads because why not? You play in a helmet and shoulder pads, so why not work out in front of the people who will decide your future in one?

Out of the 65 throws, only three landed incomplete. He threw passes coming from under center, on the move to his left and right. He connected on deep throws down the sidelines. He showed scouts how to handle pressure in the pocket. His quarterbacks coach, George Whitfield, grabbed a broom and tapped Manziel with it when he attempted some throws. If there were any questions about Manziel, he wanted them answered. Manziel's objective was to show he could make all the NFL throws. He needed to throw on the move, he needed to throw 20 yards down the field. He needed to show he could stay in the pocket and deliver a pass. He needed to hit receivers on timing routes. He needed perfection. These Pro Days are about perfection because any slip up can hurt the draft stock of a player. "I felt like it was good," Manziel said after the Pro Day, according to the Associated Press. "Obviously going for perfection, so had a couple balls hit the ground. One was on me. One was a little bit high. I could've got it down for him a little bit."

When the Pro Day was over, Manziel, like the showman he was, thanked NFL representatives for attending his showcase. He shook as many hands as he could.

Perfect.

Was it enough for the Cowboys to draft him despite what they had in Romo?

The day of the draft, Jerry and Stephen Jones talked again about what to do with the No. 16 overall pick. Jerry Jones agreed Barr, Donald, Shazier, and Martin were the top of the list. Manziel was also in the top five. "Any one of those players I'm happy with," Jerry Jones said in the meeting recalled by Stephen Jones. "We need to get better on defense. We don't even need to worry about Johnny. We're not going to take him. But let's talk about Johnny."

It was typical Jerry Jones. Let's not talk about a player, but then let's talk about it. It wasn't a passive-aggressive way of going about your business, yet it was the only way Jones knows how to go about his business. He wants to make sure the decision is what's best for the Cowboys.

The night of the draft went as expected, at least at the top. With the No. 1 overall pick, the Houston Texans selected South Carolina defensive end Jadeveon Clowney. The top quarterbacks in this draft started with Manziel. Yet it also wasn't a strong quarterback class. Derek Carr, AJ McCarron, Teddy Bridgewater, Blake Bortles, and Tom Savage were considered the best quarterbacks. Jimmy Garoppolo was also getting mentions from scouts and front-office personnel as a quarterback to watch.

Manziel had the name. He had stats. The Heisman Trophy.

Jacksonville picked Bortles from Central Florida with the No. 3 overall pick. It wasn't a stunner because Bortles had fine credentials. In three seasons at Central Florida, he threw for 7,598 yards with 56 touchdowns and 19 interceptions. NFL.com gave Bortles a 6.80 grade, which meant a Year One quality starter. Nolan Nawrocki, the NFL.com analyst, wrote of Bortles: "Big athletic, ascending quarterback with enough arm talent and intangibles to develop into a franchise starter. Is not yet a finished product, and scouts' opinions vary on his ceiling, but elements of Bortles' skill set compare to some of the best in the game today, and his best football is ahead of him."

As the first round unfolded, two of Manziel's college teammates went before him. Tackle Jake Matthews went No. 6 overall to the Atlanta Falcons, and wide receiver Mike Evans went No. 7 to the Tampa Bay Buccaneers. One of the Cowboys draft targets, Barr, went No. 9 overall to the Minnesota Vikings. Donald, another target, went No. 13 to the St. Louis Rams. Shazier was picked No. 15 by the Pittsburgh Steelers.

The Cowboys were on the clock.

Several years after this draft, Stephen Jones talked about trusting your draft board. Between all the meetings and watching of college players, that grade was the ultimate sign to where a team felt about a player. You have to trust the draft board. "I just think that's why we've had the success we've had in the drafts," Stephen Jones said. "We've tried to get ourselves in a position going into the draft via free agency that you just don't feel like you have to do something. At the end of the day, I think the discussion was outstanding. Of course, it comes up. Maybe one player may scratch an itch a little better as a need than the next guy. But at the end of the day, everybody went back to what our mantra has been around the Cowboys the last 10 years."

That comment came the day the Cowboys selected wide receiver CeeDee Lamb in the first round in 2020 instead of a defensive player. At that particular time, the Cowboys stuck with their board and drafted the highest ranked player on their board.

Back in 2014 Jerry Jones—sitting at the head of the football-shaped table with the Cowboys star in the middle with his son, Stephen, along with Garrett, the head coach beside him—posed the question. *Who do you take?* Jones was wearing a blue suit with a black tie and white dress shirt. Everyone in the room had a tie on for the most part. This was a business meeting.

Each NFL team gets 10 minutes to decide who to select in the first round. "Nobody really wants to take him," Stephen Jones recalled of Manziel's name being mentioned. "A lot of issues. A lot of things going on. I don't think anyone wants to take him."

NFL.com gave Manziel a 6.40 grade. Nawrocki's report of Manziel said, "will be a starter within the first two seasons." But this was also in the report: "A very unique, run-around, ad-lib, sandlot-style quarterback who consistently won games playing a brand of fast-paced, jailbreak football that often goes off script and can be difficult both to gameplan with and against. Is most comfortable on the move outside the pocket where he can find open throwing lanes and see the field and will command mush rush and extra spy defenders. Has defied the odds and proven to be a great college-system quarterback but still must prove he is willing to work to be great, adjust his hard-partying, Hollywood lifestyle and be able to inspire his teammates by more than his playmaking ability."

Jerry Jones asked the room of scouts, coaches, and front-office personnel about Manziel. The room was quiet. The clock was ticking. Standing behind Jones were two scouts, wearing white shirts with a tie and no sports coat. To Jerry Jones' right was Garrett. To his left was Stephen Jones. All the power brokers were at the head of the table. To the left of Stephen Jones, sat McClay. The voice of reason was at the owner's left. Stephen Jones joked that everyone had their heads down as if hiding under the table was a better option than speaking up to Jerry Jones. "Who are we going to take?" Jerry Jones said.

"I think we should take Zack Martin," Stephen Jones said.

"I wanna take Johnny Manziel," the dad said. "We talked about this."

The clock was ticking.

McClay, the vice president of player personnel, spoke next. "He's got a ton of issues," McClay said in the meeting.

Scouts talked about Manziel's off-the-field issues. Manziel liked to party. He liked to drink. He was a college kid but also someone an NFL team needed to rely on. "Why didn't we just take him off our board?" Jerry Jones said.

In reflecting on Manziel's issues, Stephen Jones felt his father made a valid point. But Manziel was on the board. "Not a leader," Garrett said.

The clock was ticking.

Phone calls were coming in. Did the Philadelphia Eagles want Manziel? They had the 22nd pick overall. Would they consider moving up? "We're always going to go by our board," then-Eagles coach Chip Kelly said. "I love him, I think he's a dynamic quarterback. I think we have a very, very good quarterback situation, not only with Nick [Foles], but you add Mark Sanchez in, Matt Barkley. We think quarterback is a strength for us right now. We felt like the pass rusher, who we had rated higher, was the guy we were going to take."

More phone calls were coming in. A bank of phones sat in front of the Cowboys power brokers. Stephen Jones slammed the phone down as if it was a wrong number. A trade couldn't be made.

Chris Hall, the Cowboys college scouting coordinator, sat in the war room ready to call Robert Blackwell, the Cowboys' representative in New York. Hall informed Blackwell of the selection. Hall had two names ready: Martin and Manziel. "Martin was a much better player," a Cowboys personnel man said. "And so I think it was just Jerry, saying, 'I'm a wildcat. I'll take a chance.' But Stephen called him off. It's pretty quick, and I think he let it be known he was really considering it because Jerry knows how to play with the media a little bit. I don't think it was that serious."

So how good was Martin? "He was a 52-game starter at Notre Dame," Garrett said. "Thirteen games a year for four years. He's been a left tackle for them but played inside at the Senior Bowl and did a very good job there. People believe he can play center, and a lot of people argue he can play all five spots on the offensive line. Initially, we will give him a chance to work inside as an offensive guard and see how he holds up there. Again, he got very favorable reviews from the Senior Bowl with him working inside. He does have a lot of position flex and a lot of experience playing outside. We feel like he can play across the board on the offensive line."

During those Senior Bowl practices, there was just one man who beat Martin in one-on-one drills: Aaron Donald.

Martin was a left tackle at Notre Dame, and the Cowboys had one in Smith. The projection was to move Martin to guard, where he could become a massive upgrade to the unit that finished the 2013 season. Ronald Leary, an undrafted prospect, started 16 games at left guard. The team signed him when questions about his knee gave other teams concerns about his long-term health. Signed in free agency, Mackenzy Bernadeau was the right guard but a player the Cowboys could move on from. There was also the possibility Martin could replace veteran starter Doug Free at right tackle. Martin's versatility was great.

As the Cowboys debated in Irving, Manziel sat in New York with family waiting. Draft picks sit in the green room at Radio City Music Hall watching the draft unfold on flat screen televisions. They get phone calls from their agents as family and friends sneak a peek on who's calling. Manziel looked nervous because other names were coming off the board. Two college teammates were gone. One quarterback was already taken. Manziel sat next to his agent, Erik Burkhardt. The media love affair with Manziel to the Cowboys was about to get an answer.

"Zack Martin?" Stephen Jones said.

"I guess," Jerry Jones said.

Hall called Blackwell and told him to pick Martin.

This dream of playing in the NFL was going to happen for Manziel but not for the Dallas Cowboys.

When Martin's name was announced in Radio City Music Hall, the site of the draft, Manziel smiled.

It was a forced smile but a smile.

The 2012 SEC Offensive Player of the Year wouldn't play for the Cowboys. He had to move on. The Cleveland Browns would eventually trade up with the Eagles to draft Manziel 22nd overall. When Manziel's name was announced for the Browns, he was on his cellphone. The crowd screamed in approval, and after Manziel hugged his family, he got an NFL draft pin placed on the lapel of his suit. He walked to the stage with a smile, took a Browns hat, met NFL commissioner Roger Goodell, and posed for pictures.

The dream of playing for the Cowboys was over. Browns owner Jimmy Haslam wanted Manziel maybe as badly as Jerry Jones. Haslam told his front-office people Manziel was the man he wanted from the start.

The Browns were in a quarterback desperation mode. From 2007 to 2014, six different quarterbacks led the Browns in passing. Dallas was in a different phase. It had a quarterback in Romo. Now it just wanted to protect him.

Jerry Jones has been there before. He didn't want to lose Romo but loved Manziel. A Cowboys draft party at Cowboys Stadium was met with mixed results when Martin's name was announced. There were boos—frustrated voices from fans thinking the Cowboys messed up the draft.

But there were few high-fives in the Cowboys war room in Irving after Martin was picked. It was a sense of relief. "Everybody felt so strongly about Zack," McClay said in the Cowboys' *Deep Blue War Stories* documentary. "I give Stephen credit for being extremely strong because Jerry was extremely strong."

Yes, the team had Romo, but the Cowboys owner and general manager looked at what Manziel could bring to the table. "No one knew to be excited with Jerry's demeanor," Stephen Jones said of the war room scene.

The Cowboys made the right move by sticking with their draft board over an item with potential problems.

So did the Cowboys have a chance to trade down from the No. 16 overall pick? "There were technically some firm offers," Jerry Jones said. "But not anyone that we were interested in."

So the Cowboys bypassed moving down via potential trades as the clock wound down on them so another team could get Manziel. Maybe moving away from a trade meant the Cowboys wanted Manziel more than they're letting on. "The fact that we got Romo more protection with that quality of player took any of the positives," Jerry Jones said. "There's no way any of the quarterbacks comes in here and beats out Tony Romo. We know that. There we had an outstanding starter that could really come in and immediately come in and help us do what we needed to do. I said the other day we are strong at the quarterback position in our minds, and the fact that Martin was there mitigated any consideration or a lot of thinking about whether or not you ought to go with Johnny. As you well know in here, Romo is by contract, as well as by commitment, is certainly the quarterback for the Cowboys for several years to come. There is no moving around that. I don't care who you draft; that's the way it would have been. That was going through our minds from the get-go. That's why we didn't spend a lot of time at all in this draft considering Manziel."

That line, saying they didn't spend a lot of time talking about Manziel, is interesting in itself, considering Jerry Jones brought up the quarterback's name in meetings. It was met with swift resistance by some in the organization because the need to get Martin was so great, especially the way the Cowboys wanted to rebuild their offensive line with younger, more talented players. "We believe games in the National Football League are won up front," Garrett said. "If you look at the best teams in the league now and for a lot of years, they are able to control the line of scrimmage on the offensive side of the ball. We did that for years here when we won championships here in the '90s. You need to build the infrastructure of your team, and we feel like we've got a great start with that with Tyron Smith and added to that last year by drafting Travis Frederick. We feel like Zack Martin is in that same mold of those kinds of guys. We feel like he is a darn good football player. When we evaluated him against some of the other guys all across our draft board, he consistently came up as one of the best players in this draft. We had an opportunity to get him at 16, we felt like it was important to be disciplined. We felt like we had needs going into this draft. You want to address your needs, but you want to address your needs with the best players available. We felt like we did that today."

Martin was an innocent bystander in the Manziel discussions. The Cowboys held a draft party for their fans in Arlington, the site of their stadium, and Manziel's name was chanted before the pick.

Martin wasn't in New York sitting in the green room watching the draft. He was home. "I was actually up in my parents' bedroom with my parents and my two brothers, so it was really quiet up there," Martin said.

It was a safe pick over someone with a troubled college lifestyle with the skills to play in the NFL.

Is Zack Martin the man who would be known as the player drafted over Johnny Manziel? "That's fine by me. I can live up to that," he said.

This wasn't a sexy pick. Some draft picks rarely are—given where a team is located in a particular round.

Where Martin ended up along the offensive line was a small issue for the Cowboys. He could play all five positions. He wasn't going to the left tackle position with Smith there or the center position manned by Frederick. "It's just kind of a reps thing," Martin said after being drafted. "If you switch sides, it's just getting used to the different. Foot is back, and if you move inside, it's just everything is a little closer. So, I've gone over those techniques throughout my career, even though I didn't

Zack Martin prepares to fire off the line in 2021, a season in which he made 16 starts to earn his seventh Pro Bowl nod.

play there. I'm looking forward to playing in the spot they put me in."

There was no controversy in drafting Martin. Just find a place along the offensive line for him to play. Manziel was the pick everyone wanted. It didn't matter how much the Cowboys tried to deny it, but Jerry Jones thought it was a good thing. "I'm just looking at it today," Jones said. "You put that with the Dallas Cowboys, and you put that with a quarterback controversy over Romo, and you've got an explosion. Manziel said it better: 'it's just bigger than you could take.' There's no question that was there. More important than anything, I do believe he's going to be outstanding in the NFL as a quarterback. Gosh, who was a guy who really did some good stuff? Garcia, Jeff Garcia, who had a little bit of that but who could develop a way to turn it into mobility for passing, who had a lot of the same build. Obviously, Manziel is quicker and instinctive. I don't want to build him up and take anybody down. But there is no one in looking at him who didn't think that they would be hard-pressed to name anybody who has had better instincts at that position. He's got a chance to knock it out of the park, and we all know that."

Romo was QB1, and his status within the organization was strong, yet Jerry and Stephen Jones talked to Romo about the possibility of drafting a quarterback. It didn't bother Romo.

The move to draft a quarterback, if done, wasn't meant to replace Romo; it was to bring depth.

Manziel was more than depth. Manziel was Manziel. "During that time more than anything, you're excited about adding a football [player] and a guy who can help your football team," Romo said. "The organization has done a great job of going about the process of getting some people on the defensive and offensive lines that can help change the football game, and that's ultimately a difference...in our way that we're drafting now, and it shows we're committed to that. And that's how you win in the National Football League."

Drafting Manziel would have led to many outside of the organization to think Jerry Jones runs the draft. And in theory he does but not without the informed conversations with his son and other front-office personnel. Garrett and McClay had powerful voices with the Jones family when it came to free agency and the draft. If there were concerns about selecting Manziel, and there were many, then McClay and Garrett would say something about it.

There weren't such concerns with Martin. "At the end of the day, we are going to put him in and mix him into the competition we have up front," Garrett said. "And we are going to be a better offensive line, a better offense, and we will probably play better defense the better we play on the offensive line. We will be able to run the ball better and control the football a little more. We just think he is a darn good football player. I'm really excited to have him on our club."

It just seemed like the right thing to do on all levels. The Cowboys had draft needs for defense—hence the look at Barr, Donald, and Shazier. But Martin also gave the Cowboys strength along the offensive line. Manziel was a luxury item. He was a pick the Cowboys really didn't need. "I knew what our team was hoping for in the draft and so I think it was a great time to look at some of the top players that were available," Romo said. "And I knew we had a couple of guys up there, and Zack was one of those guys, and once he was available, I knew we were really excited about him. It's great that we got a guy with his ability at that spot in the draft, and I think it's going to show it's going to be a really good draft when it's all said and done."

Jerry Jones felt drafting Martin was a statement the franchise was settling and not telling its fanbase they wanted elite players. "He really respected the room," Stephen Jones said of his father.

It was a difficult situation for Jerry Jones, a man used to getting his way. But Jones wouldn't be the man he is without compromise and not hiring people he trusted to help him in the decisions for his football team. Jones trusted his people, especially his son, when it came to free-agent decisions. When the Cowboys released Hall of Fame wide receiver Terrell Owens after the 2008 season, it was Stephen Jones pushing for it for the betterment of the team.

So a frustrated Jerry Jones, wishing for Johnny Football and the sales that came from Manziel's jersey No. 2 in Cowboys gift shops, was gone now.

When the Martin pick was made, Jerry Jones left the war room briefly to decompress. It was his way of coming to grips with what was going on with his franchise. Deep down he knew the decision was proper. As the first round of the draft neared a conclusion, Jerry Jones grabbed his son in a headlock and said, "I love ya, we did the right thing."

If there was ever a player the Cowboys didn't need to draft it was Manziel. His career was one misadventure after another. He played just 14 games for the Browns before off-the-field issues pushed him out of the league. It was a waste of talent and an example of how scouting a draft prospect's character influences whether a team will select him. In later years Manziel admitted he didn't take the NFL seriously, particularly the preparation part of it.

Martin, however, was the perfect draft pick. As the Cowboys rebuilt their offensive line, Martin was the final piece when he was selected in the first round in 2014. Dallas got Smith for left tackle, Frederick for center, and Martin at right guard. Martin was named to seven Pro Bowl teams and is a five-time All-Pro. He was named to the All-Decade team in 2010.

8

SECOND-ROUND PICKS

THERE ARE SUCCESS stories when it comes to the NFL draft. It's easy to target first-round selections. Some of the best players ever drafted in league history came with the No. 1 overall pick. You can look at Peyton Manning (Indianapolis Colts in 1998), Orlando Pace (St. Louis Rams in 1997), and Troy Aikman (Dallas Cowboys in 1989). Those three players were Hall of Fame players where projections from talent evaluators worked.

Later in those first rounds, teams have found talent—only to have other teams think about what might have been. Aaron Rodgers of the Green Bay Packers remembers the 21 NFL teams that bypassed him, including the Minnesota Vikings and Dallas twice, before he was selected 24th overall in 2005. Patrick Mahomes of the Kansas City Chiefs was the 10th overall selection, and many question now why he fell. What about T.J. Watt of the Pittsburgh

Steelers? The pass rusher fell to No. 30 overall in the same draft as Mahomes. What happened to that evaluation?

Von Miller was the second overall pick in 2011 by the Denver Broncos. The No. 1 pick by the Carolina Panthers was Cam Newton. Is it easy to second-guess the decision by the Panthers looking back on how successful Miller is? Maybe the third pick of the NFL draft should have gone to Patrick Peterson instead of the Buffalo Bills selecting defensive tackle Marcell Dareus. The Arizona Cardinals ended up selecting Peterson at No. 5 overall. The second-guessing is fun, easy, and complex.

Weighing a team's needs versus best player available is always a difficult task for NFL executives. A coach can get in the way sometimes of finding the best talent. A scout or general manager can feel strongly about a player but won't say anything to the team owner, who ultimately has final say on all draft picks. And while team owners have the final say, a majority allow the general manager or highly valued personnel director to make the call on a draft pick.

Several teams will have a head coach with tremendous power make a final decision on a draft pick. A coordinator can have influence on who a team should select if a tiebreaker is required in the war room. You could say drafting NFL players today is an archaic task when new ideas are needed. But the NFL draft remains an unpredictable business.

Scouts tour college campuses on weekends of the fall to evaluate talent. Cowboys owner and general manager Jerry Jones said he values that end-of-season grade on prospective draft picks because that's the first real informed opinion on whether a player is good or not.

The Cowboys under Will McClay, the vice president of player personnel, have a two-tier system of grading players. The area scout will present a grade on a player, and then a national scout will follow up with a grade. The goal is to have every draftable player seen by at least two scouts over the course of a season. It might take two seasons to compile the true grade of a player who has been scouted in person.

These are not easy decisions but are needed to push a franchise from rebuilding mode to title contender. One of the hardest jobs is evaluating a player coming off injury. A player is projected as a first-round selection, but an injury could derail everything. It puts a player and an NFL team at risk with the unknown of whether said player can live up to his potential. An injury could be considered minor by one team and not another. During the NFL Scouting Combine, NFL teams bring team doctors and trainers to examine prospects and ask questions about their injury history. Draft reports will sometimes have a player's injury report from high school. It could be a minor injury such as an ankle sprain his sophomore season that prompted a scout to write something up based on a conversation he had. That minor injury can also determine the toughness of a player. Did he play through the injury? Yes, in high school.

In the college game, the pressures to play through injuries are paramount. It can also set the tone for a player as a professional. Former Cowboys wide receiver Amari Cooper has told the story when he played at Alabama how he tried to miss practices and games with a minor injury. Alabama coach Nick Saban didn't force Cooper to play. It was Saban's reaction to Cooper sitting out that changed everything. "It wasn't in the pros. It was in college when I was banged up," Cooper said. "I didn't always know how to play hurt. Just mentally, the physical pain was never really a thing. It was just the mental part. Mentally, I used to be like, *Dang, if I'm 100 percent, I'm just so much better obviously than when I'm hurt.* That kinda played a part in it being a mental stumbling block for me. Saban, he put another guy in front of me cause I kind of kept taking myself out the game, and it just messed up the continuity of everything. So now I just I'd rather play hurt than to be switching with a guy in there. I just started playing hurt, and then what happened was I started having my best games when I was hurt. It was crazy. I'd be healthy, I'd have good games, but I'd be hurt with real pain, just fighting through it, and I'd have my best games. So from there, I was like, *Man, maybe I need to be hurt some more.* That's just how the cookie crumbles sometimes, man. When you least expect something to happen, it happens. That's just how life is."

Playing injured is part of the NFL world. It's really part of this sport we call football.

But college players with dreams of participating in the NFL can see injuries derail careers. It can also give careers a slow start. Several of the best players in league history were projected as first-round picks, but an injury pushed them out of the first round. Some NFL teams don't want to take a chance on selecting a player coming off an injury. The NFL game has no time for patience. Coaching jobs are on the line, and waiting on a prospective first-round pick that fell in the second round and has his availability in question isn't worth the risk.

But some NFL teams will take that risk, hoping a particular player can thrive once he's fully healed from the injury. All it takes is one team to give an injured player a chance, especially when he recovers from the health issues. Some players when healthy are productive to the point where a first-round grade isn't a second-guess. But it's a risk. You must be secure in the front office and coaching staff to take such a chance on a player. Trusting the science of the medical staff is another part of the equation. If the medical staff doesn't believe a player can perform at an elite level once recovered from injury, there's no sense in taking a chance.

That's why the medical teams attend the Combine to give evaluations on players. Sure, the player will say he's fine to not only the team doctors and coaches and front office personnel, but also to the media at large. Player agents will also present a positive outlook on a client's recovery. There is no need to be negative when coming off an injury. Some players hate talking about injuries when trying to enter the draft, knowing every little thing can disrupt the draft process. It doesn't matter what a player did on the field for three seasons; if he suffered an injury his final year or the year before, scouts want to see skill work at the Combine and Pro Days.

If a player displays speed on the field, but an injury ends his final season in college, then scouts want to know when the player is going to work out. Unfair? Of course, but it's the NFL, and the ability of players to perform at an elite level—or just a competent level—is all teams are looking for. A nick on the draft report when it comes to an injury can push a player's grade from a second-round pick to a fifth-round pick. And if a player is able to perform in workouts after recovering from injury, does he look the same before the injury?

You could say NFL teams are paranoid. That's fair. Team executives answer to NFL owners who invest billions to purchase franchises. These are gambles that some teams are willing to take more than others. It's best to avoid a player coming off an injury in college because why wait a year for that player to develop into what you want.

NFL teams want to give second contracts to draft picks. It says the evaluation of the player was sound because the team wanted to keep him. The salary cap dictates a lot of what a team can do, but you want quality players to warrant second contracts after drafting them. NFL teams can hold onto a player for five to seven years if he's a first-round pick or four to six years if he's picked in the later rounds. Most contracts are five years for first-round picks and four years for second- through seventh-round picks. If a player is talented enough, but a team can't work through a contract extension, a franchise tag can be administered in consecutive seasons.

Some players hate the franchise tag because it restricts their movement. Another NFL team can match the tag, but it would have to give up first-round picks to obtain a player. It's rarely done, but the maneuver is available if need be. When it comes to college players coming off injury, franchise tags are just a dream. The hope of just trying to get drafted to prove to NFL teams they can play after recovering from injury is the goal.

NFL teams want these players to succeed because they put their trust in the medical staff and the coaching staff's ability to maximize the potential. Players hate talking about injuries.

Coaches believe it's bad luck to speak about it as well. In the reality of the dirty game of the NFL, talking about injuries is something that must be done. It's a reason, outside of the betting lines, why NFL teams present an injury report distributed by the league three times a week during the regular and postseasons.

The Cowboys have encountered their share of players who overcame injuries to get drafted by their team. Some found success while others just could never recover to fulfill their potential. It's a gamble to draft a player coming off an injury because the risk is so high. Yet, the type of injury and the makeup of the player says a lot about why the risk is worth it.

SEAN LEE WAS a star high school football player at Upper St. Clair in Pittsburgh. He was a safety, running back, and an excellent basketball player. But in Western Pennsylvania, if football is your first love, then you play football. And if a college projects you to play linebacker, then you attend Penn State. Lee picked Penn State over Iowa.

Why wouldn't he go to Penn State to become a linebacker? The school is nicknamed Linebacker U for a reason. Jack Ham, Greg Buttle, Matt Millen, Andre Collins, Dave Robinson, Shane Conlan, LaVar Arrington, Paul Posluszny, and Dennis Onkotz are some of the great linebackers from that school. Lee wanted to be one of those linebackers.

He played in eight games his freshman season in 2005, and after that it was difficult to keep him off the field. He started 13 games in 2006 as a sophomore, but it was the 2007 season where everything changed for Lee. It was a 138-tackle season, in which he earned All-American honors, All-Big Ten honors, and the Defensive MVP of the Alamo Bowl. When the 2007 season finished, Lee thought about turning pro. There was no question about his skill set as a strong tackler who was physical and had the intelligence to attack ball carriers. He wasn't a fast linebacker, but his quickness and his ability to recognize plays were a strength.

However, NFL teams projected Lee as a second-round pick, and he decided to return for a senior season. "I put my papers in, and they came back second-round grade, whatever that means,"

Lee said. "I was planning on staying. I always wanted a senior year at Penn State. I had great senior year in high school that I cherished with my friends and I wanted the same experience at Penn State. I think I got that."

With Lee returning for his final year of college, he prepared for the 2008 season with spring practices. But Lee suffered a torn ACL in his right knee in a non-contact drill in April of that year. It was a simple drill, something Lee had done countless times. It was a delayed blitz where Lee waits for the ball to be snapped, and then as the quarterback is just into his dropback, he sprints to the pocket. He was unblocked and made a quick cut and suddenly he went down. "I was more in shock," Lee told the *Pittsburgh Post-Gazette* a week after the injury. "I said, 'I can't believe I tore it. I can't believe I tore it.' I was bummed at that point. There was no contact at all. I can't believe it happened on a play like that. I keep looking for a reason why."

There is no why. Sports are cruel. Winners and losers only. People lose jobs for losing. Winning is what matters. Lee understood that. He wanted to return to Penn State. Yes, his draft stock wasn't what was expected. There is nothing wrong with a second-round selection, but Lee's final season at Penn State would have likely gotten him to the first round. But leaving Penn State after that kind of injury wasn't happening. So he did the best thing he could. He jumped into the rehab program at Penn State and sought to return stronger.

Lee had to get over what had just occurred to him. He also needed support. Lee's sister, Allie, tore her ACL while playing soccer and underwent surgery herself two months before Sean Lee's injury. "It's kind of an inspiration to me to see how well she's done," Lee told the *Post-Gazette*.

Later in the interview, Lee kept talking about the hows and whys of his own injury. He took out an insurance policy against career-ending injuries, something most prospective NFL prospects do. Lee, though, planned to suit up again for Penn State. "I'm coming back," he said. "I want to play another game. I want to prepare for another game in the locker room. I want to play another game in this stadium. I can't see myself not doing it. I'm definitely going to try to be back."

Lee was able to get a medical redshirt so he could play a fifth season at Penn State. For Lee, it was everything he desired: the goal of playing with teammates one more time before, of course, playing in the NFL. He was going to become another linebacker from Linebacker U to reach the NFL. In 2009 Lee returned. After compiling 86 tackles—47 solo—he was named second-team All-Big Ten.

He wore a brace on his right knee, which raised concerns with NFL scouts. The other issue for Lee was that he sprained his left knee and missed three games. Now the clean career he thought was going to happen was getting clouded with health problems. He entered the NFL draft with problems to both knees and wore a brace on the right one. Before he participated at the NFL Scouting Combine, Lee shed the knee brace and worked out for teams. "Especially after the last two years, I have to show them I'm healthy," Lee said at the Combine. "I went through all the medical stuff and I want to prove to them that I'm healthy and I'm going to work out and that my knees and legs are 100 percent."

Lee displayed a 37.5-inch vertical—a solid accomplishment from a talented high school basketball player—and 4.71 speed in the 40 along with 24 reps on the bench press at the Combine. At his Penn State Pro Day, Lee ran the 40 in 4.60 seconds. There was no need to showcase anything else. Lee had proven to people he returned from two years of injuries: a torn ACL in the right knee and a sprained knee in the left.

Yet, questions remained. There always are. "I'm sure it's a concern for teams," Lee said. "The last two years, I wasn't nearly as durable as my first three years, but I'm here to prove I'm 100 percent. I could play right now. I'm sure a lot of these guys are going to have injuries in their career. The difference between me and them is: I've had them, I've come back from them and proved I can play through them. You can look at it as a plus, especially considering I'm healthy right now."

Who was going to take a chance on Lee? During the draft process, Lee worked out for the Dallas Cowboys, New York Giants, Arizona Cardinals, Pittsburgh Steelers, Cleveland Browns, Atlanta Falcons, and Indianapolis Colts. Lee felt he was a first-round talent. He showed he could come back from an injury. The worst injury he ever had was a torn ACL. It happened in college. So if you're going to suffer a health issue, why not get it out of the way while you're still on a college campus.

Gambling on the health of an NFL player is a tricky business in a sport where millions are at stake. Lee understood the risks involved for NFL teams, but he believed he was healthy. He believed he could play injury free in the NFL. All he needed was someone to believe.

The 2010 linebacker class of the NFL draft wasn't very strong. If Lee didn't have health issues hanging over him, he might haven been included among the best linebackers coming out. Rolando McClain from Alabama was considered the best linebacker coming out and he had first-round projections surrounding him. Sean Weatherspoon from Missouri, Sergio Kindle

Sean Lee mans the linebacker position during his 11th and final year with the Cowboys in 2020.

from Texas, and Koa Misi from Utah were also first-round projected players. Lee was also among the players considered for
the second or third rounds.

The Cowboys valued Lee. Head coach Wade Phillips understood what it meant to have a durable linebacker in the middle
of his 3-4 defense. But the Cowboys had other projections going
on. Wide receiver Dez Bryant from Oklahoma State was getting
strong interest from teams. If you thought Lee's health issues
made his stock drop, Bryant's off-the-field issues—from an eligibility problem costing him his final year in college to behavior
questions—was forcing Bryant's stock to slide.

Yet, some NFL teams loved Bryant's talent. He was a physical
receiver who could take over a game. Jones knew he needed an
infrastructure around Bryant to keep him out of trouble. There
was a trust level between Jones and Bryant's agent, Eugene Parker,
about what the franchise could do for Bryant. The wide receiver
needed guidance, and Parker was hopeful the Cowboys would
draft him. Jones would later say several teams bypassed Bryant
due to his perceived off-the-field issues. It seemed NFL teams
crossed the line when it came to Bryant.

The Miami Dolphins general manager at the time, Jeff Ireland,
asked Bryant if his mother was a prostitute. Ireland apologized for
asking the question, but the lack of sensitivity was clear when it
came to Bryant. *What does Bryant's mother have anything to do
with his ability to play in the NFL?*

Some would say nothing. NFL teams might think it has something to do with his upbringing that explains his wayward ways.

When the 20th pick of the 2010 NFL Draft approached, the
Cowboys selected Bryant. It was a joyous time for Bryant because
he wanted to play for Dallas. He watched the draft from the house

of his mentor, David Wells, in a Dallas suburb. The next step for the Cowboys was finding a linebacker.

The inside linebackers for the 2009 Cowboys were Bradie James and Keith Brooking. The two veterans were backed up by Bobby Carpenter, an underachieving former first-round pick from 2006. Phillips was confident in Brooking and James returning as starters in 2010, but Brooking was going to turn 35 in October of 2010. At some point, finding a younger replacement, considering the team was less enthused with Carpenter's future, was important.

Here sat Lee.

McClain was the best linebacker in the draft and he went in the first round (No. 8 overall) to the Oakland Raiders. Weatherspoon was snagged by the Falcons at No. 19. The Cowboys were targeting Lee but weren't sure if obtaining him was possible. When the team selected Bryant, the next step was looking at the highest-ranked players remaining on the draft board. Jerry and Stephen Jones are always working the phones. With the first round ongoing on a Friday night, talking trade with teams continued for future rounds.

On Day Two of the draft, the Cowboys sought a trade partner for Lee. Dallas ended up trading up with the Philadelphia Eagles, moving from No. 59 to No. 55 in the second round. Dallas also gave up a fourth-round selection (No. 125 overall) to secure Lee. Three inside linebackers went off draft boards in the middle of the second round, and that's when the Cowboys felt good about where Lee would reside.

The injury factor was heavy. He missed a senior season with a torn ACL and in his fifth year he was absent for three more games with a sprained knee. Both knees had issues. He played his fifth

year with a knee brace. The questions about Lee's health were legitimate. Dallas believed in Lee and wasn't afraid to take a chance.
If the Cowboys were going to select Bryant in the first round,
considering his off-the-field issues like attitude with coaches and
whether he wanted to study the game, then getting Lee was easy.
So Lee was picked in the second round.

When it was time to pick, Lee was the highest-ranked player
on the Cowboys' draft board despite his health concerns. "It's a
case of doing what you should be doing," Jerry Jones said the
day Lee was selected, "really reading your board and looking at
real distinctiveness as opposed to trading down and going toward
need. Sean Lee was that."

The health issues didn't scare the Cowboys, and it kept Penn
State's tradition of Linebacker U secure. The 2010 draft marked
the first time in 18 seasons that three Penn State linebackers were
taken in the same class. In addition to Lee, NaVorro Bowman
was drafted in the third round (91st overall) by the San Francisco
49ers, and Josh Hull was drafted in the seventh round (254th
overall) by the St. Louis Rams. Lee's health neither stopped him
nor Linebacker U.

THE MOMENT IT happened it left you crushed. Jaylon Smith was
playing linebacker for Notre Dame. He was a team captain, a
projected high first-round selection. He hadn't decided if he was
going to turn pro, but family from his native Fort Wayne, Indiana,
knew. He was gone.

All he had to do was play one last game: the Fiesta Bowl
against Ohio State.

This game meant something to Smith. He was playing against the school that finished second in his college recruitment. He was also playing against the team of his brother, Rod, a former running back at Ohio State.

Smith had been coy with reporters leading into the game about whether he was going pro. Smith's family took out an insurance policy in case he was hurt. That way, if something happened to him, some sort of financial gain would be obtained.

But a family doesn't get insurance policies hoping for something to happen. Smith was pushing for the NFL. He had been the best high school linebacker in the nation. After 39 starts over three seasons, the NFL advisor board told Smith he was good for the first round. "It's something that sticks out," he said before the Notre Dame–Ohio State game. "I want to be great in everything I do. So I definitely wanted it to be all first-round [grades]."

This was his expected final college game. Teams couldn't wait to draft the 6'3" 220 pounder from Bishop Luers High School in Fort Wayne. This was a perfect way to end a college career: major bowl game in an NFL stadium with everybody watching. Smith knew he was turning pro. There was nothing left for him to prove at Notre Dame. He just wanted to play one final game. He was a team captain. He was the leader of the defense. Forget that. He was one of the leaders on the team. He was a well-liked, intelligent football player. Smith always had a mind for business. Once he turned pro, he was hopeful the money he made would lead to something bigger. Football was his life. But football didn't define him. Yet, football was a means to success financially and in celebrity.

One more game is all he wanted.

With eight minutes left in the first quarter, the world changed for Smith. Ohio State quarterback JT Barrett faked a handoff and darted up field on a read-option. It's a play where the linebacker uses his eyes. Watch the ball. Watch for the handoff. Watch the quarterback. Watch the running back. Barrett faked the handoff to running back Ezekiel Elliott and went to his right. Smith watched Elliott and stood flat footed but was blocked to the ground before he could react. Barrett had just completed a long pass to tight end Marcus Baugh.

Ohio State went into hurry-up mode. Notre Dame's defense remained on the field waiting for the next play. When it happened, everything changed. Barrett fumbled the ball as he was going to the ground. Sensing this, Smith moved to his left. As the ball was being recovered, Ohio State tackle Taylor Decker made a slight push, then another, and Smith went off-balance toward the pile, but the landing was a crash. His left leg bent in a way no human's leg should. Just before hitting the turf at University of Phoenix Stadium, Smith grabbed his leg. *Hamstring? Cramp?* Not even close.

Smith hit the ground in pain. He laid on his back and quickly took off his helmet. Trainers quickly rushed to him. The entire Notre Dame defense stood around him. They stood wanting to protect him. They stood, knowing what this game meant to him and what his future stood to look like. Team captain, safety Matthias Farley, yelled, "Fuck!" as he left the field.

Sheldon Day and Romeo Okwara, two defensive linemen, waited for Smith to get up. He couldn't. Elliott stood alone. He was the only Ohio State player waiting for Smith to stand, which Smith could not. Elliott walked off slowly and tapped Smith's chest gently.

Notre Dame coach Brian Kelly approached the two trainers talking to Smith, who was despondent. He knew. The trainers knew, too. The exact extent of the injury wasn't known. All that was certain was Smith needed help off the field. He couldn't put pressure on his left leg and he eventually left the field. Smith's final game of his college life was over and not in the projected way he envisioned. It was over due to injury.

He returned to the sidelines with his knee wrapped and on crutches. You could see his face, soul searching for answers. After the game won by Ohio State 44–28, Kelly said it was a significant knee injury. "The guy is so impactful on our defense," Kelly said. "You lose a guy like that early on, it significantly affects what you're doing defensively."

Smith was not only Notre Dame's leading tackler, but also the winner of the Butkus Award given to the nation's best linebacker. It didn't matter now. Doctors determined there was nerve damage to his left leg, particularly in the foot area. He tore ligaments in his ACL and LCL. Tearing ligaments can be repaired, but nerve damage may never recover, and if it does, it will certainly take time.

The injury occurred in January. The NFL draft was in April. Smith was determined to be ready for an NFL season that fall. But that wasn't going to happen. If a team was going to select Smith, it had to know about the injury. It had to know his recovery might take two years. *Who wants to wait two years? Who even wants to wait one year?*

Smith, though, was confident he would not only get drafted, but also play. "Oh, that's the goal. As soon as possible," he said. "I can't tell when I'll be back, but I'll be back 100 percent."

Working out at the NFL Scouting Combine and the Notre Dame Pro Day wasn't going to happen that spring. During the

Combine interviews, NFL teams examined the knee. *Would he even play again?* Just before the Combine in late March, Smith said he just started walking. Smith was in denial about the nerve damage. "No, the nerve wasn't stretched at all," he said. "It's just the healing game. That's all. It's a process. I'll be back 100 percent. We just don't know when."

Smith had peroneal nerve damage. He had lost feeling in the foot and needed to wear a brace. It's a brace to keep the foot upright—just so he could walk. This brutal game had taken Smith from playing in the pros. Smith, though, was resilient. "It's the game of football and it happened," he said. "I have no choice but to live with it. I'm just moving forward. That's all I'm focused on."

Doctors told Smith he could play football again. They couldn't tell him when. This severe injury would cost him a first-round selection, maybe more.

The man who pushed Smith during the Fiesta Bowl was remorseful. In the buildup for the NFL draft, Decker was asked about his actions.

It wasn't a dirty play. It was a football play. "After it happened, of course, you don't want to injure somebody to that degree," Decker said to the *Detroit Free-Press*. "Football is a physical, violent game. I just wanted to reach out to him and wish him all the best. And he told me right back, he's like, 'No hard feelings at all.' So I think that was really mature of him. And I played with his brother at Ohio State, so I wish him all the best. He was a hell of a player when we were watching him on film, so I think, hopefully, he'll battle back from it and he'll be good to go."

Smith wasn't mad at Decker. He wasn't mad at anybody. He just wanted to play, and this injury was going to delay it.

The Dallas Cowboys understood the severity of Smith's injury. Dr. Dan Cooper was the Cowboys' team physician and he performed the surgery on Smith a week after the injury. Cooper came highly recommended by Smith's agent, Eugene Parker, whose relationship with the Cowboys was deep. Parker trusted the Cowboys, and Smith trusted Parker. Cooper explained the issues with Smith's injuries. It wasn't so much the knee because athletes have ligament damage all the time. "[Smith's nerve is damaged] enough to make it go to sleep, but it wasn't stretched enough to be structurally elongated or visually very damaged," he told *USA TODAY*. "He's had time for his nerve to regrow two inches, and the area of where his nerve was injured is six inches above the muscle that it innervates. I wouldn't really expect him to get much innervation back into that muscle for two or three more months. Then once it does—I've seen kids who are completely paralyzed like him on the lateral side and not able to pick their foot up at all [that] wind up being totally normal."

In reality there was uncertainty about Smith's return. But the Cowboys felt confident if they drafted him that they had the doctor, Dr. Cooper, and the proper rehabilitation staff led by Britt Brown to help him return. It was a big if.

Smith wasn't falling down draft boards. He was being taken off them. Why should a team draft him if it's hard to determine when he'll play again?

When the 2016 draft approached, Smith wanted a party. It was a scary time because if nobody picked him, then embarrassment would occur. But Smith had faith he wouldn't get embarrassed. He had faith somebody would take a chance. When the first round started, some of the players Smith played against and with in his last college football game were going off the board. The first were Ohio State teammates Joey Bosa at No. 3 and Elliott at No. 4. Smith's teammate at Notre Dame, tackle Ronnie Stanley, was gone at No. 6. Ohio State cornerback Eli Apple went No. 10. Then the man who put Smith in this position, Decker, went No. 16. Ohio State linebacker Darron Lee was picked at No. 20, and Notre Dame wide receiver Will Fuller was picked right after that at No. 21.

Meanwhile, Smith was hosting a draft party with his family. He sat with friends waiting for a phone call. And then his iPhone rang. "Dallas, Texas. Dallas, Texas," he whispered to a friend.

"Jaylon? Will McClay, Dallas Cowboys, I got somebody who wants to talk to you," the Cowboys vice president of personnel said from a black office phone located in the Frisco, Texas, Cowboys team facility.

"Jaylon, this is Jerry Jones with the Dallas Cowboys," the team owner said.

"How you doing," Smith said as he started to jump up and down.

"We doing fine, and it's great to be talking to a Dallas Cowboy," Jones said.

"Yes, sir, thank you so much," Smith said, trying to fight through tears. As the call progressed, family members surrounded Smith. "I appreciate you so much. I appreciate you so much. Thank you so, sir."

Head coach Jason Garrett then took the phone. "You're going to love it here," Garrett told Smith while the noise at Smith's draft party grew.

Smith lost his first-round pick status when his injury pushed him into the second round. But at least Smith was valued by someone. "It's been the most challenging time of my life," Smith said. "But at the same time, it's been the best time where my dream has just come true. I've been wanting to play in the NFL since I was seven years old."

MEL RENFRO'S LIFE swirled like a tornado. He was a highly-sought draft pick from Oregon, a two-sport star in football and track and field. He was a two-way player on the football team as a halfback and defensive back. Renfro said he knew during his junior season that the NFL was calling for him. The NFL was in his future. He was slated as a first-round pick. Life was good.

Well almost.

While he was thriving on the field, his wife, Patricia, was pregnant, and they were separated. Renfro was in his early 20s, trying to figure out his maturity as a man, husband, and soon-to-be father. He was also about to move.

There were no NFL teams in Oregon. (He was born and raised in Houston until the family moved to Portland.) His exploits in the early 1960s on athletic fields were documented with praise. In 1960 the *Capital Journal* in Salem, Oregon, reported that Renfro helped his high school, Jefferson High, win the A-I title. He set state records in the board jump at 24¼ inches and in the low hurdles at 18.9 seconds. He was named to the High School All-American team by *Scholastic* magazine. Renfro was a star in high school, and it carried over to college.

But then his future was unsettled. Sure, he was going to play in the NFL. It was just trying to figure out when.

Then, on November 22, 1963, president John F. Kennedy was assassinated in Dallas. Renfro was in an apartment with teammates, watching the black-and-white footage of what was occurring that tragic day. It set up a world of emotions. "I just got frustrated, and [we're] drinking beer," he recalled years later. "I don't know. I have some company that came in and I just didn't want to have any company and I just took a bottle there and threw it up against the wall."

Upset that the country was in civil unrest due to the racial climate at the time, Renfro then went into the bathroom. "I

Former second-round pick Mel Renfro poses during 1973, the year he made his 10th and final Pro Bowl.

slammed my hand up against the mirror in the bathroom," he said, "cut my wrist pretty bad."

Just before he smashed his hand, his wife, Patricia, who was nearly seven months pregnant, walked in. "I didn't expect her to see her pop up in the apartment," he said. "I was just kind of frustrated. She walks in, she's there, I'm frustrated. So I go into the bathroom, and in my frustrations—so, it's blowing off steam—just banging my head against the wall and bang, bang my hand against the mirror, which was the big mistake. It did cut my wrist pretty bad."

Renfo's teammates said he needed to go to the hospital, but he refused. His hand kept bleeding with no end. His teammates began to worry. So did Patricia. It wasn't about the NFL anymore for Renfro. His life was at risk due to the amount of blood on the floor of the bathroom.

His teammates were scared. He started to get scared. All of a sudden, common sense took over. The emotions of what was going on around him began to subside. He finally went to the emergency room to discover he had torn a tendon in the wrist. He lost the feeling in two of his fingers. Once a projected first-round pick, Renfro said the rumor mill said he cut his entire wrist off and would never play football again. Renfro knew better. Doctors stitched him up and said he could play football again.

But there were issues with NFL teams. Dallas Cowboys executive Gil Brandt developed a relationship with Renfro from his time scouting college players. During a college visit, Brandt made sure he was stranded at an airport in Oregon just to speak with Renfro alone.

When the draft occurred that year, the Cowboys held up the second round for nearly 10 hours. Brandt later said that Renfro was the man they wanted, but they needed doctors to examine him. Doctors cleared Renfro. It was a bad cut, but nothing that prevented him from playing football. In fact, there was a college All-Star Game that summer coming up for draft prospects, and Renfro was expected to participate.

But several NFL teams didn't know the severity of Renfro's injury. The Cowboys knew and they drafted Renfro in the second round. Renfro said it was a blessing. He recovered physically from the injury and renewed his relationship with his wife. The frustrations of his personal life, the pressures of becoming a professional, and the death of a beloved president took a toll on him. "I was a young kid. Where would I be now?" Renfro said. "I may not have been a Dallas Cowboy, and my whole life would have been different, not growing up in Dallas, or being in Washington D.C., or being in Philadelphia, being in New York and New Jersey. It's a scenario that could have happened if I had not cut my hand."

Renfro and Patricia would have two more kids but would divorce years later. The relationship remains strong to this day. But life away from football affected Renfro where he couldn't suppress his feelings any longer. "It's part of what happens," he said. "There were a lot of repercussions."

Renfro's plummeting draft stock falls didn't prevent him from reaching the Pro Football Hall of Fame. In a 14-year career, Renfro reached the Pro Bowl in his first 10 seasons. He led the NFL with 10 interceptions in 1969 and was a two-time Super Bowl champion. Despite the concerns over the wrist injury, Renfro ended up being one of the Cowboys' most durable players and an elite talent.

Jaylon Smith didn't let his leg injury stop him either. He missed the 2016 season while still recovering from the nerve damage, but he practiced and played with a foot brace, which he eventually ditched. Smith, though, always knew his career was going to be short because there was no telling when the nerve damage would return or when the trauma to his leg would ultimately lead to losing his lateral movement, something he utilized to become a highly sought after draft pick coming out of Notre Dame. He played only five seasons, earning a Pro Bowl berth in 2019, and the Cowboys signed him to a contract extension. He was a well-respected player in the Cowboys locker room. When Smith was released in 2021, defensive coordinator Dan Quinn read an inspirational speech to the team.

Sean Lee's health issues never left him. Whether it was a torn ACL that cost him the 2014 season or hamstring problems in the latter part of his career, Lee's health was regularly a question. Yet, Lee was a two-time Pro Bowler and considered the heartbeat of a defense during an 11-year career. He recorded more than 100 tackles four times and became a mentor to several younger linebackers, including Smith.

9

DAK PRESCOTT

DEZ BRYANT STOOD on the sidelines with his hands up. The white chalk from the football field covered both arms like leeches getting comfortable with the taste of his skin. The Dallas Cowboys wide receiver was trying to understand everything around him and maybe years from now he will. Maybe not.

A 31-yard reception was taken away from him and his team. He was pleading with side judge Rusty Baynes for answers. "I tried to reach over the goal line," Bryant said through the roar of the crowd. Bryant was pleading. If he was in a smaller room instead of a loud stadium, he would be screaming at Baynes. Instead, his demeanor wasn't threatening; it was of desperation. Baynes was either not listening or couldn't hear Bryant's plea for answers. A decision was made, and Bryant's reaction was of devastation. Bryant thought he caught one of the biggest passes of his career and maybe started a deep playoff run the Cowboys hadn't seen in more than 20 years. It was the start of the end.

On January 11, 2015, Dallas played the Green Bay Packers in an NFC Divisional Playoff game in Lambeau Field. The Cowboys and Packers are two iconic franchises in the NFL with fanbases and television ratings to prove it. A Cowboys victory meant it could move into the next round of the playoffs, the NFC Championship Game, a place it hadn't reached since 1995. A potential victory also would have revealed the end of mediocrity under coach Jason Garrett. The Cowboys finished 8–8 in Garrett's first three full seasons as head coach.

In this 2014 season, Garrett finally got this Cowboys team into the postseason. And with that came increased expectations. The National Football League is a cruel place. When things are going well for you, something happens, and only the best teams survive the adversity the league presents itself on a weekly, sometimes daily basis. Just when the Cowboys were finally going somewhere with Garrett, the cruelty of what sports does to you slapped the franchise in the face.

This was the end of Tony Romo.

Nobody really knew it during this game. How could they?

The Cowboys quarterback was having a Pro Bowl-type season. He led the NFL in completion percentage at 69.9 and in quarterback rating at 113.2. After a three-interception game in the season opener against the San Francisco 49ers, Romo would go on a seven-game stretch where he threw 14 touchdowns with just three interceptions. His completion percentage was 69.3 percent, and he had a quarterback rating of 111.4. That seven-game streak would end when he fractured two small bones in his back in an overtime loss to the Washington Redskins. But Romo finished the season strong, leading the Cowboys on a four-game winning streak where he threw 12 touchdowns with just one interception as the offense averaged 41.3 points per game.

Romo and the Cowboys offense finished the 2014 season seventh in total yards (6,138), third in yards per play (6.1), and second in rushing offense (2,354 yards). After convincing the organization to rebuild the offensive line, Garrett had a football team that could finally play complimentary football.

Romo was at his peak in this road playoff game with a chance to beat his favorite team growing up: the Packers. Romo was raised in Burlington, Wisconsin, a two-hour drive south of Green Bay. Romo, while admiring Hall of Fame quarterback Brett Favre, would also say John Elway, a Denver Broncos Hall of Famer, was a quarterback he idolized. In truth, Romo is a cheesehead. Fans in Wisconsin rooted for Romo as a pro—not over Favre—but rooted nonetheless. But when you play with the star on your helmet, being a cheesehead doesn't matter anymore. Here was Romo's opportunity to knock off the Packers.

It was his last chance. He just didn't know it.

Legendary Lambeau Field is a perfect venue to win a game against the team you grew up rooting for. The history of Lambeau Field dates back to the first game in 1921 when the Packers played in what was called the APFA, the American Professional Football Association. Lambeau Field opened in 1957, costing $960,000 to build. A victory for Romo against the Packers in such a historic place would have been the biggest win of his career.

It wouldn't happen. Yet Romo tried. Bryant tried.

The Cowboys trailed 26–21 when Romo took this team to the Packers 32 with 4:42 to play in the game. It was fourth and 2 when the Cowboys lined up for the game-on-the-line play. Romo saw Bryant matched up toward his left one on one with Packers cornerback Sam Shields. It's a matchup the Cowboys believes they could win. It's their best receiver against the Packers' best corner. Skill wise, Bryant's physical presence should overtake a smaller defender such as Shields. Romo knew this. So he threw a sideline pass to Bryant, who outjumped Shields to the ball's highest point down the Cowboys sideline.

That's something scouts want to see in wide receivers. Can you reach a ball at its highest point? When prospective NFL prospects attend the NFL Scouting Combine or college Pro Days, scouts measure vertical leaps. So all those measurements came into play on this cold day in Green Bay where Bryant was trying to secure a pass in a game the Cowboys desperately needed.

Bryant made his sideline catch and landed near the 1-yard line. Shields was hanging on to Bryant, trying to tip the ball away. Bryant reached out for the goal line, but the ball got loose as he landed. He was ruled down at the 1. "You the baddest motherfucker on the planet," Cowboys wide receivers coach Derek Dooley said to Bryant on the sidelines after the catch. "If we don't score here, you got to do it again."

On the opposite sideline, Packers coach Mike McCarthy challenged the play. He knew the rule. When you catch a ball, it must be secured all the way down to the ground. If the ball moves in your hands, it's not a catch. If the tip of the ball touches the field, it's not a catch. McCarthy threw the red challenge flag, knowing, hoping he would get the call.

The Cowboys sideline was perplexed. "Should be a touchdown," Bryant said loudly on the sidelines. The cold weather dried out Bryant's lips. They were chapped. His skin was deadly cold. He was yelling. He was begging. He was pleading. "That's a catch," he yelled.

Years later, McCarthy went into detail on why he challenged the play. "I had one timeout, maybe four minutes left in the game," McCarthy said. "And I said after the game, 'That was one hell of an athletic play.' I was impressed. Dez and Sam Shields, you're talking about two great athletes going after the football. But I asked the question in regards to how the rule was written and I was given the right answer by the referee. So then I challenged it."

McCarthy had second thoughts about challenging the play until he spoke with referee Gene Steratore. That discussion changed McCarthy, and the red flag got tossed out.

During the review the referees watched the replay of the catch as a majority of the crowd of 79,704 waited for the fate of this game. If it's ruled a catch, the Cowboys get the ball at the 1 with an easy chance to take the lead. If ruled incomplete, the Packers get the ball with an opportunity to run the clock out. "It was a great catch, I can say now," McCarthy, who is now the Cowboys head coach, said laughing. "But it wasn't then, technically."

The fourth-down completion was overturned, and the Packers got the ball and eventually ran the clock out for the victory. There was no laughing in the Cowboys locker room. Shock. Misery. Confusion. "I don't understand why it was even a challenge," Bryant said in the locker room nearly an hour after the game. "Have you ever seen that rule before?"

Bryant and Romo were robbed of going into Cowboys' lore as heroes. There are two catches in franchise history that place this franchise on opposite ends. Dwight Clark caught a touchdown pass over Everson Walls in the 1981 NFC Championship Game to clinch a Super Bowl berth. It was a pass Joe Montana would say later he was just trying to throw away. Drew Pearson caught a Hail Mary from Roger Staubach to beat the Minnesota Vikings in a 1975 NFC Divisional Playoff as a snowball was thrown at him.

And now we have a non-catch for Bryant and Romo.

The 2014 season ended. Aaron Rodgers, the quarterback for the Packers, secured the victory as the offense ran out the clock. Not only did the clock end this game, but also Romo's time with the Cowboys.

It happened so quickly and suddenly that the Cowboys were almost unprepared for it.

How could a franchise prepare for losing their starting quarterback? Few NFL teams have elite quarterbacks as backups. The Cowboys had Staubach and Craig Morton to choose from in the 1970s. The 49ers had Montana and Steve Young in the 1990s. Having two elite quarterbacks happens to NFL teams, but at some point, those teams have to make a decision on a full-time starter. Staubach took over for Morton. Young replaced Montana. Mostly, NFL teams utilize journeymen or young prospects sitting around, waiting for QB1 to go down, retire, or in some cases, get replaced. There was no replacing Romo.

Jerry Jones wanted Romo to play forever in his dreams. He didn't believe Romo was old. Why would he? Romo entered the 2015 season at 35. Not too old, not too young. Perfect. But sometimes the human body betrays you at certain points of your life. It leaves you speechless and a franchise scrambling. The Cowboys felt they weren't there yet.

But in the second game of the 2015 season, Romo suffered a broken left collarbone. Philadelphia Eagles linebacker Jordan Hicks sacked Romo, landing hard on the quarterback causing a break.

Romo was done.

Not for the season but until he was healed completely. There was no guarantee the collarbone wouldn't be damaged again. He missed seven games as Brandon Weeden and Matt Cassel tried to save a failing 2015 season as the backup quarterbacks. A chance for the collarbone to get fractured again was a real possibility. Doctors cleared Romo to play, but you can't blame the organization for being concerned.

It's easy to second-guess any decision, and Romo was healed. His body was telling him he could play again. In his return, on November 22, 2015, he completed 18-of-28 passes for 227 yards. He was sacked twice. He threw two touchdowns and two interceptions in a 24–14 victory against the Miami Dolphins. He returned, and everything was fine.

The next week everything changed. Again.

Romo was sacked by Carolina Panthers linebacker Thomas Davis on the last play of the third quarter, and the collarbone broke again in the same place. The season for Romo was over now, and the Cowboys lost four of their last five games. "It was one that kinda [kept] breaking," Romo said in an interview with Graham Bensinger years later. "We finally figured it out, but by that point, I was well on my way to talking like Graham Bensinger."

What Romo meant was retirement. He didn't know it yet, but it was coming.

Jones is the ultimate optimist. If a player is hurt, he's got the faith the player can heal. It's like he's got a special room where he visits a higher power to ask for healing of his players. In 2016 Jones had that faith his starting quarterback would finish out the season. He didn't worry about health issues with Romo anymore.

People inside the organization knew better. Maybe this was it. Romo knew it too back then. He just didn't say it until years later in that interview with Bensinger when he was retired.

The Cowboys window with Romo was closing.

Dak Prescott finished his 2015 season at Mississippi State in the Belk Bowl in Charlotte, North Carolina. Mississippi State had defeated North Carolina State 51–28 as Prescott threw four touchdown passes. He completed 25-of-42 passes for 380 yards.

Prescott's aunt was sitting in the stands watching the game with an NFL executive. It was by happenstance. Tad Prescott, Dak's older brother, remembers the ending of that day. "She happens to be sitting close to the Cardinals GM [Steve Keim] at the time who told her, 'Yeah, I'm here both watching Dak and [N.C. State quarterback] Jacoby Brissett and after the game tell him we're coming to get him. We'll be having drinks in Arizona. Drinks are on you.'"

Tad Prescott wasn't sure what to think of the NFL draft. His brother was confident he would go in the second or third rounds, which is Day Two. Dak Prescott felt he was good enough to not just play in the NFL, but also to start. To lead a team. His confidence was fostered by four seasons at Mississippi State where in his senior season he set career highs in passing yards (3,793) and touchdowns (29). He threw a career-low five interceptions.

Prescott's on-the-field life is built as an underdog. He wasn't considered the starting quarterback when he attended Haughton High School in Haughton, Louisiana. Prescott eventually took over the starting job when the starter suffered an injury that allowed Prescott to emerge as a three-star recruit, according to recruiting services Rivals.com and Scout.com. But despite leading his high school to an undefeated regular season in 2010, where he was named first-team All-State, he didn't receive a lot of college offers. He was considered a dual-threat quarterback, a man who uses his legs and arms to get an offense down field.

Mississippi State was perfect for Prescott because it ran a majority of its plays in shotgun formation. Prescott threw for 2,860 yards and rushed for 951 yards, combining for 39 touchdowns that senior season of high school. Only LSU, TCU, and Mississippi State offered scholarships. Prescott picked Mississippi State.

He redshirted that freshman season in 2011 and the next year saw limited playing time. In 2013 as a sophomore he shared the starting job with Tyler Russell. But in 2014 Prescott exploded onto the college football scene. Prescott took over the starting gig when Russell suffered a concussion. "I've started at every level the exact same way unfortunately," Prescott said years later when he was in the NFL. "For these guys, unfortunately, high school, college, now the NFL, I became the starter—cause of injury."

In 13 starts he broke 12 school single-season records and finished eighth in the Heisman Trophy voting, the highest of any player in Mississippi State football history. As a dual-threat quarterback, Prescott broke school records for rushing yards by a quarterback with 986 yards and in total offense with 4,435 yards. He led his school to their first Orange Bowl appearance in 73 years.

The next season Prescott picked up 4,381 total offensive yards with 39 touchdowns. He led the SEC with 226 completions, 2,528 passing yards, and total offense per game at 363.2 yards in conference games. Prescott became the only player in the SEC to lead his team in passing and rushing yards. The resume Prescott put together was impressive. He didn't play like a three-star recruit. "I'd say he might be the best player I've ever coached. If you look at my coaching resume, that's pretty impressive," said Dan

Mullen, Prescott's coach at Mississippi State who went on to become the head coach at Florida.

NFL teams were impressed with Prescott's leadership ability. He earned an undergraduate degree in educational psychology in December 2014 and the following year earned a master's degree in workforce leadership. Prescott was a people person. He learned how to speak with people because that's what a quarterback has to do.

Prescott's personal life humbled him, too.

Prescott's mother, Peggy, died of colon cancer in 2013. With Dak having grown up with two brothers in a trailer park in Louisiana, his mother was everything to him. Peggy Prescott worked at a truck stop to put food on the table. "Like many of these young guys, the football field is their safe place," Prescott's high school coach Rodney Guin said in an interview with NFL Network. "The football field is where they are most at home and most comfortable. It really just shows the job his mom did and how she raised him and the character she helped instill in him. Mom was very hard on him, wanting him to do well and where they could be successful in life. She worked very hard, a great, great lady. She'd want to be the one you want to interview if you could. It would be something else."

It was that hard work that Prescott admired in his mother, and he wanted to honor her every moment he played. On his left wrist, there's a tattoo that says "mom." "When you lose your mom, it's not that easy," Prescott said to FOX Sports in 2018. "That's something you've got to wake up every day, looking yourself in the face, and knowing that you've got an angel. You've got an angel that has expectations for you to do and you've got to go out there and do them each and every day."

At Mississippi State's Senior Day, Prescott was introduced to the crowd, holding flowers for his mom, an angel in heaven. He hugged Mullen and several others, including his two brothers and grandmother. When he got to his father, Nat, a strong embrace occurred, and the two men started crying. Dak and Nat looked up into the sky and pointed upward. It was an emotional moment for Prescott, a self-described "momma's boy" who felt the pain of not experiencing the last two seasons of college football with his mother around.

With his greatest moments as a football player occurring without the mom who nurtured him, it was an emotional time for him. It was something NFL teams admired. The compassion he had for people—not just teammates—but anyone.

Yet, NFL teams had questions.

In 2015 Prescott, along with two teammates, were involved in a fight in Panama City, Florida, while attending a concert of rapper Waka Flocka. Prescott was a bloody mess after he was jumped by several people at the concert. He wasn't arrested. From a legal standpoint, he didn't do anything wrong. "He didn't initiate it, and, hell, any man would defend himself," said a Cowboys executive at the time Prescott was being evaluated for the NFL draft. "So I don't think it was a negative or even a positive that he got into a fight."

In 2016 Prescott was arrested for a DUI for which he was later acquitted of any charges.

So any of the perceived character issues NFL teams could place on Prescott were minor. NFL teams felt this was a good guy with high character.

A prime example of this was in high school. Kyle Brister was a high school assistant for the football team. Brister was autistic.

Brister's duties were washing the uniforms, getting footballs, and other small duties. After Haughton High School won its 10th game of the season, Prescott said the team should carry Brister off the field on their shoulders. It was Prescott wanting to acknowledge the importance of Brister regardless of how small his job was compared to the other coaches and staff members of the team. So once again, character wasn't a problem for Prescott. How could it be?

The Cowboys didn't really need him, but quarterbacks coach Wade Wilson saw something in Prescott. In the spring of 2016, Prescott participated for the South Team in the Senior Bowl. It's an All-Star Game for college prospects where the two teams are coached by NFL coaches. The Cowboys coached the North, and the Jacksonville Jaguars coached the South. Though Prescott's interaction with Wilson was short during the week in Mobile, Alabama, where the Senior Bowl is held, Wilson took a liking to Prescott. The quarterback completed 7-of-10 passes for 61 yards and one touchdown in leading the South over the North 27–16.

Wilson and the Cowboys met with Prescott again at the Combine in Indianapolis. He impressed them again not only in the meetings, but also with his on-field work. The biggest issue was Prescott's inability to work under center. The league was changing to having more quarterbacks—especially those with the ability to make defenders miss—work out of shotgun, but Prescott still needed to show teams he could work under center. It wasn't something that was considered an end-of-the-world type of thing because most—if not all—NFL coaches believe they can fix a player's deficiencies.

Prescott said he first took live snaps under center at the Senior Bowl. "I'm athletic. It's not that big of a transition," Prescott said at the Combine. "It's kinda funny, but I almost feel like a big-time quarterback from under center. It's something that I'm embracing and having fun and getting comfortable at."

Prescott visited numerous teams during the draft process. He had dinner with Keim in Arizona. He felt good about the visit with the 49ers. But the visit to Dallas was special. Jones remembers it well. "Wade Wilson went down and worked him out at Mississippi State. We had him in our building and spent a lot of time with him," Jones said. "We spent a lot of time with a number of the different quarterbacks. You go down and you figure out where you want to put those guys on the draft board, and when it comes time to pick one of those names, it is a very thoughtful process to lead you there. Obviously, we value the quarterback position. We wanted to get a young, developmental guy in here, and he was a guy that we really liked as a person. We liked him a lot as a player, highly endorsed by everybody at Mississippi State. His career speaks for itself, and there is a lot to like about this guy. A developmental quarterback that we think is going to fit in well to our system."

Wilson told Jones that Prescott walked down the hallways of The Star, the Cowboys practice facility, like he owned the place. Wilson told Jones he was like a Pied Piper.

There were two problems with Prescott: Romo and other quarterbacks.

Romo was QB1 coming off an injured-filled season, but Jones was confident in him. The Cowboys liked two other college quarterbacks in Paxton Lynch, a 6'7", 244-pounder from Memphis, and Connor Cook, a 6'4", 215-pound quarterback from Michigan State. Lynch and Cook bore the look of how old-school traditional quarterback are supposed to: big, tall, with strong arms. Yet, the leadership of Prescott was off the charts.

Dak Prescott, who readies to throw during the 2021 playoffs, was an incredible value pick, having been selected 135th overall in the 2016 NFL Draft.

Cook and Lynch couldn't compare, especially with the way Prescott played. He was a dual-threat quarterback in high school and college. With the NFL game going to more mobile quarterbacks, he seemed to have an advantage over other quarterbacks with less mobility. "Tyrod [Taylor], Cam Newton, Russell Wilson, they have all opened the door for the mobile quarterbacks," Prescott said. "The guys who are making throws from under the center in the pocket, doing the things they need to do within the pocket but as well as stretching the defense and using their mobility to really hurt the defense."

The Cowboys roster not only had Romo, but also Kellen Moore as the backup, so whoever the team was going to draft, if that became a possibility, the expectations were low that player would play.

Day One of an NFL draft is boring if you're not expected to have a team call you. It's a Thursday night geared for the top prospects of the NFL draft and where draft experts find out how accurate their mock drafts truly are. Cell phones buzz with agents receiving calls from team executives and scouts about what's happening with their clients. Sometimes you really don't know what to believe. It's not like teams are lying; they just don't know. It's an educated guess about who will get drafted and where, and Prescott wasn't sure because nobody really knew. "We sit through the first day, just watch the draft. Everything is expected," Prescott said. "We hit that second day, and that's where you can start to see the anxiety start to sit in."

As the Prescott family waited, the Cowboys didn't. The Cowboys had the fourth overall pick of the NFL Draft and selected running back Ezekiel Elliott from Ohio State. Despite the love from Coach Wilson and offensive coordinator Scott Linehan on

Prescott, Jones loved Lynch. After the Cowboys drafted Elliott, a desire to get back in the first round became paramount as Day One of the draft moved along.

The Seattle Seahawks had the 26th overall pick in the first round, and team officials received several phone calls. The main calls were from Dallas and Denver. If the Cowboys were secure in QB1, the Broncos weren't.

Mark Sanchez and Trevor Siemian were the main quarterbacks on the Broncos roster. Sanchez was a failed first-round pick, having been the fifth overall selection by the New York Jets in 2009. Siemian was the Broncos' seventh-round selection in 2015. Broncos officials were also interested in signing former 49ers quarterback Colin Kaepernick. He was a talented quarterback, but his protesting of police brutality against people of color and raising awareness to social ills by kneeling during the playing of the national anthem irked many team officials in the NFL. The Broncos seriousness in signing Kaepernick, a free agent at the time, was questioned. But here during the draft, is where Elway, the Broncos general manager, decided to make a play for Lynch.

He was competing with Jones for Lynch.

Dallas made calls to at least nine teams to move into the second round. The most serious talks came with Seattle. The Seahawks didn't need a quarterback, having employed Wilson. Yet, the Cowboys were looking for a quality backup on their depth chart, and Lynch was the target. A fury of calls came flying with Seattle on the clock. Seattle owned the 26th pick of the draft and requested a second-round pick from Dallas (No. 34 overall) and a third-round selection (No. 67 overall). Jones, as is his custom, polled the room of scouts, coaches, and personnel people. Should two draft picks be used to acquire Lynch? The

Cowboys would have the future QB1 in Lynch should something happen to Romo.

Stephen Jones, the Cowboys executive vice president, was against giving up two picks to enter back into the first round. A counteroffer of a fourth-round pick along with the second-round selection felt best. In more of a desperate need than Dallas for a quarterback, Denver gave Seattle what was desired. Denver gave up its first-round pick (No. 31 overall) and a third-rounder (No. 94 overall) to Seattle. Deal. With Denver moving up five spots to get Lynch at No. 26, it gave the Broncos a possible future quarterback and ended any discussions for signing Kaepernick.

In Frisco, Texas, the site of the Cowboys practice facility and team headquarters, Jerry Jones second-guessed himself. He went home after Day One of the draft and couldn't sleep. He regretted not doing something at a position he felt needed improvement. "I got to bed about 3:00 [AM] thinking about the Lynch thing, got up at 6:00 [AM], and before the morning was over had talked to six people about how I messed it up," Jones said during the draft. "I was still mad about it the next morning."

Jones felt the third-round pick was worth it. In the minds of many in the front office, it wasn't.

What was so special about Lynch? He was 6'7", a tall quarterback with a powerful arm. He started 38 career games at Memphis and threw for 8,863 yards with 59 touchdowns. Both stats ranked as the second most in school history. Before forgoing his final year at Memphis, he led the Tigers to a 19–7 record in his sophomore and junior seasons where his team went to bowl games. It was the first time since the 2007 and 2008 seasons that Memphis went to consecutive bowl games. "When I look back on my life, I've overpaid for my big successes every time, and when I've tried to get a bargain or get a little cheaper or get a better deal on it, I ended up usually either getting it and not happy I got it or missing [it]," Jones said. "I probably should have overpaid here."

Day Two of the draft is on a Friday afternoon. It's two rounds—second and third. Projected starters at skill positions such as linebacker, cornerback, tackles, safeties can go in these rounds. Players with first-round skill sets fall to these rounds due to injuries or character issues. And sometimes teams just miss out on prospects in the first round where a talented player falls. "Second round goes by, then the third round completes, and his name hadn't been called, and you can kinda see he's upset now," Tad Prescott said. "And he's trying to figure out what's going on, especially with the other guys that were taken in front of him."

There were six quarterbacks taken in the first two days of the NFL draft. The first two picks were Jared Goff and Carson Wentz. Brissett, the quarterback who lost to Prescott in the Belk Bowl, went 91st overall to the New England Patriots. Wentz played in the Senior Bowl with Prescott and had an uneven performance, which raised concerns about whether he should be a top pick.

There was no major draft party at Prescott's house. It was just family watching the draft that day. But there was concern on the third day. "The whole process is just about at that point keeping his mind off the draft," Tad said. "Let's go fish, let's go have a few drinks, let's do anything we can that's not concerning ourselves with this draft. Of course, the next day comes; [it's] the same thing. You could just see it on his face because he was really quiet that day. That was the first day of the draft of the entire time we'd had been there that he was actually really quiet. He didn't talk to anyone. He wasn't speaking to [younger brother] Jace or myself.

The day before, we had been playing basketball. He wasn't about that. He was completely locked in on this draft."

Saturday morning the Cleveland Browns started the fourth round with two picks. The Browns had the No. 99 and No. 100 selections. The Cowboys had No. 101. This was the Cowboys' next chance to get a quarterback. Cook was the highest-rated quarterback on their draft board. He was available if the right price was met. With Prescott and his family waiting for something to happen, Jerry Jones and the front office tried to do it. Not for Prescott. Dallas wanted to get pick No. 99 from Cleveland.

So did the Oakland Raiders. "The fact that we didn't get him there—don't interpret that as much with as hard as we worked on Lynch," Jones said. "Those were different intensities, different stakes."

The Raiders offered a fifth-round pick (No. 154 overall) along with pick No. 114 to move up to No. 100. Done deal. So Cook, a player the Cowboys valued over Prescott, was going to play in the AFC West instead of the NFC East.

During the draft, phones can buzz and cause disruption. A family member asks what's going on. A friend or a girlfriend seeks answers. "He finally gets that phone call and he was freaking out because he thinks it's the 49ers because that's who is on the board at that time and he was a huge Niners fan at the time," Tad said. "And he's jumping and running around the room. *Oh, he's going to the 49ers* and all this and then, of course, he's on the phone, and I don't know who he's talking to. Even when he says, 'Coach Wilson,' I have no idea who he's talking to. I have no idea who is on the phone with him and who he's talking about, and then, of course, that's when he says, 'Jerry Jones,' and I go, 'Oh crap!' That's the Cowboys and that was his dream. I lost it."

A house filled with family and friends watched Prescott take the call. He's sitting on the couch wearing a black baseball hat. He sounded calm as those around him were ready to scream. He said "yes, sir" a few times. His grandmother held his hand. It's hard to determine who is drafting Prescott until he said, "I have Coach Wilson's number."

Then the room erupted in excitement. A woman wearing a gray Cowboys T-shirt smiled proudly. Prescott hugged his grandmother, and then the room went silent again. There's a television in the upper corner of the room, and everybody was listening. There's a hush over the place as two men introduced themselves over the television. In the middle rounds of the NFL draft, teams have fans or ex-players announce draft picks. Hall of Fame offensive lineman Rayfield Wright was sitting with John Trevino, president and general manager of Telemundo, a Spanish language television station. Wright introduced Trevino. Then Trevino made the announcement.

Prescott knew he was going to the Cowboys. But you want to hear it. You want to feel it. You want to know that it's real. Once Prescott's name was announced, the room exploded again, and Dak Prescott's father, Nat, hugged him from behind.

The Prescott brothers are close. Dak, Jace, and Tad hugged each other and started to cry. The emotions of losing their mother, Peggy, to colon cancer, bonding together, fighting to reach this point of getting drafted in the fourth round by the Cowboys had overcome them.

There were seven quarterbacks drafted before Prescott, who went 135th overall. "Lots of comps for Dak Prescott to Tim Tebow," former Cowboys executive Gil Brandt tweeted the afternoon

Prescott was selected. "But I think Dak's better prospect out of college. He has chance to eventually replace Romo."

Yeah, Romo. The QB1.

Garrett described Prescott after the Cowboys drafted him. "A great leader, positively impacts everybody there, has played big in big games, and has done a lot of really good things on the field," he said. "Physically, he is big; he is strong. He can throw it; he can run. He is a very experienced player. Again, he is developmental from the standpoint that he is young and he has to learn how we want to do things, but there are a lot of tools there and a lot of great character qualities that you love."

Coach Guin knew why the Cowboys picked Prescott. He saw it in middle school when Prescott's name was talked about more than the other kids. It was more than that bright smile of his. It was the talent on the field and a warm feeling he presented to a person to make them feel better. He wasn't Dak Prescott back then; Rayne Dakota Prescott was his full name. "Well, I think they saw maybe his ability. What they didn't see was him," Guin said. "You don't know what you're getting unless you really know him. There may have been more talented guys out there, but the person he was would outweigh his athletic ability every time."

Prescott wasn't the starter in high school until an injury gave him a chance. He wasn't the starter in college until an injury gave him another chance. Then the ultimate goal of reaching the NFL, an objective only Prescott knew was possible, was put into motion. "We have a good plan, a real good plan," Jones said. "Exciting in that his upside is about his character. He's about it. Jason [Garrett] reminded me that we have spent a couple of times in the offseason with Roger Staubach. Roger said to both of us at the same time—because he thought we were considering the future after Romo at quarterback—and he said somebody the team will really follow, that they believe in him, that they will follow him. Invariably, when you ask about Dak, that's the first thing that came out. It was that magnetism, that leadership that is involved. I don't want to write a check with my mouth that he has to cover here, but he has *it*. He does have a lot of work to do with Jason and a lot of work to do in becoming a pro quarterback. The effort has started."

Prescott was the first Cowboys quarterback drafted since 2009. "In this case I'm going to say that this could be couched as a process, but on the other hand, it's strictly as we look to the future," Jones said after the NFL draft in 2016. "All of it does add up for the future and is a cause that if Romo is healthy, he's going to play the games. What's great is if there ever is a time where we feel like we can have Romo off the field, we have someone here that can get snaps and show how he does in the NFL and how he does with the Dallas Cowboys. I think it complements us very well with what we are going to be doing with our quarterbacks."

The quarterback position is delicate. You have to withstand plenty to make it work. The Cowboys picked Prescott with no expectations he would eventually take over, but Romo's body suffered another injury in the 2016 preseason. Romo's backup, Moore, injured his ankle in training camp, pushing Prescott to the No. 2 job.

As quickly as Bryant's catch was taken away, so was Romo's job because the Cowboys drafted Prescott. Few knew it at the time.

Sometimes NFL teams find players that few teams want. Brady was a sixth-round pick (199th overall) by the New England Patriots. Brady won seven Super Bowls. Staubach was drafted four years before he was eligible to participate in the NFL due to his commitment to the armed service. The Cowboys waited for Staubach before eventually using him over Morton. The Cowboys placed high value in Lynch and Cook, but two coaches, Wilson and Linehan, saw value in Prescott.

The leadership, strong arm, and his ability to run in an NFL game, which was changing to benefit a more mobile quarterback more than a standard dropback passer, was important. When Romo took over the starting job in 2006, he was different from Drew Bledsoe. Romo had mobility in the pocket, something Bledsoe didn't have. And here came Prescott, a younger, mobile quarterback with excellent leadership skills. How could the Cowboys bypass Prescott?

His resume was excellent. You can ignore the numbers of what a quarterback does sometimes. Yet what he possesses off the field can outweigh this. Prescott had both the numbers and the leadership. NFL teams expect quarterbacks to be leaders, the face of the franchise. Whenever you draft a quarterback, that goes into the equation.

Lynch and Cook had the size—what NFL scouts call the measurables—to play in the NFL. Prescott was 6'2" and 238 pounds. He wasn't the fastest quarterback coming out of that 2016 draft and probably didn't have all the arm strength as a Wentz or Lynch and quite possibly Goff, the No. 1 overall pick that year by the Los Angeles Rams.

Prescott had something else that you probably couldn't teach. Prescott had the intangibles NFL teams seek every year in players, particularly quarterbacks. And while the Cowboys thought about drafting another quarterback, Prescott was there for the taking. At No. 135 overall, the Cowboys picked Prescott.

The next quarterback taken? Ohio State's Cardale Jones by the Buffalo Bills. Jones was third on the depth chart at Ohio State and took on a similar path as Prescott. He replaced an injured J.T. Barrett to start in the Big Ten Championship Game and eventually lead the Buckeyes to the national championship. Two other quarterbacks, Brandon Allen, a sixth-round pick by the Jacksonville Jaguars, and Jeff Driskel, another sixth-round pick, went later. Both were regarded in some ways maybe even higher than Prescott on some NFL draft boards.

Picking a quarterback is no easy task. The Cowboys wanted Prescott to succeed but had their own QB1 in Romo. Reality sets in with NFL teams. Eventually. Romo was the starter. A man not going anywhere, but Prescott wasn't going to be deterred himself. "We are totally committed to giving him every opportunity to develop," Jones said of Prescott at the time he was drafted in 2016. "You're thinking about the future here. From my perspective, it's a good time to inject him, his skill level, what he's about into our staff."

Prescott wasn't supposed to start his rookie season. He was fourth on the depth chart in 2016. But injuries to Romo and Moore allowed him to move up. Prescott never gave up the gig. Romo retired toward the end of the 2016 season, knowing it was Prescott's time to take over. In 2016 Prescott was named AP's Offensive Rookie of the Year. He since has been named to two Pro Bowls and in 2021 signed the richest contract in franchise history. Prescott's emergence calmed Jones' fears of searching for a quarterback, something he endured since Troy Aikman retired in 2000.

10

MICAH PARSONS

IT WAS EARLY January 2020 when the Dallas Cowboys conducted interviews for a head coaching job that wasn't vacant. Head coach Jason Garrett remained the Cowboys coach following an 8–8 2019 season. He spent 10 seasons with the Cowboys as the head coach, getting to the postseason three times and recording four 8–8 finishes. Despite his moderate success, the Cowboys fanbase grew weary of Garrett. When he was hired permanently in 2011, he was the next young offensive-minded coach that Jerry Jones wanted to lead his franchise back to a Super Bowl.

Garrett couldn't do it.

The reasons why any coach gets fired are complex. Losing a power struggle with a general manager or just being overmatched during a tenure are some of the issues leading to firings. This was no power struggle. It was just time to move forward. But the Cowboys didn't just fire Garrett. They let him stay on until his contract expired in early January. While Garrett knew he was out as coach, Cowboys ownership moved along with two interviews.

Garrett, meanwhile, was going to hold exit interviews with his players while the Cowboys did interviews for his job.

It was a curious way to conduct business.

Garrett felt the right thing to do was finish exit interviews with the players. But the Cowboys had an obligation, too. Garrett understood the business of the NFL and wasn't going to stand in its way. Garrett had future employers waiting to hire him. It was just a matter of when they could speak with him.

For the Cowboys opening, two men interviewed: Mike McCarthy and Marvin Lewis.

Lewis fulfilled the Rooney Rule requirement, which mandates an NFL team interview a person of color. Stephen Jones, the Cowboys' chief operating officer/executive vice president player personnel, worked with Lewis on the NFL's competition committee. The two had a good relationship so it was an easy decision to speak with him. Lewis was a defensive specialist, and the Cowboys defense sought change.

McCarthy was the other man interviewed. This wasn't a surprise interview either because McCarthy was a successful NFL coach with an extensive offensive background. During two days of interviews, Jones Jr. turned toward his father and said, "What are you waiting for?"

The elder Jones wanted to interview more coaches. Everything he heard from McCarthy sounded good. In fact, it sounded right. He decided to hire McCarthy, making it official January 8, 2020— not so much because of what his son was asking but because of what McCarthy owned: a Super Bowl ring. In 13 seasons with the Green Bay Packers, McCarthy compiled a 125–77–2 record. McCarthy coached the Packers to the playoffs for eight consecutive seasons, guided quarterback Aaron Rodgers to stardom, and led the Packers to a Super Bowl XLV victory. The Packers won that game against the Pittsburgh Steelers in Cowboys Stadium.

The resume was perfect for not only the offense, but also the team overall. The continued development of offensive coordinator Kellen Moore could flourish under McCarthy. NFL teams speak about continuity with an offensive line, and the same is said of a coaching staff. Quarterback Dak Prescott turned into a star quarterback with Moore as the quarterbacks coach and eventual play caller. McCarthy knew if he was going to get the Cowboys job, retaining Moore to work with Prescott was a priority. Instead of calling the offensive plays, a task he once held in Green Bay, McCarthy would morph into a CEO role. It was something he once despised when he coached in Green Bay.

Now McCarthy was embracing a CEO title with the Cowboys. Time management, planning the practice schedules, having input on the 46-man gameday roster and the final 53-man roster were the mandatory requirements now. What play to call on third and 2 was not.

Jerry Jones' concerns of a novice at that position was eliminated since McCarthy was a head coach with more than 20 years of experience. His first season with the Cowboys, however, was a failure.

Several things were going against McCarthy before he stepped on the field: the coronavirus shut the world down. The power of the NFL was even affected. NFL teams had to conduct the NFL draft remotely, and offseason work with veteran players on the field was eliminated. Wearing masks, social distancing, meticulous cleaning of team facilities, and meetings with medical personnel became more important than building a team.

But building a team couldn't be ignored because the NFL was determined to play games, while other sports like the NBA, MLB, and the NHL delayed seasons from continuing. The NBA moved into a bubble-like environment in Orlando, Florida, so it could complete the season. A bubble-like environment for the NFL was out of the question. It was discussed but difficult to achieve. The league was determined to play games—even without fans—because there was a commitment to its television partners. And while the league was figuring out the new world of COVID-19, NFL coaches were doing it in a different way.

McCarthy put together a veteran staff particularly on defense where he hired Mike Nolan as the defensive coordinator. On paper hiring Nolan was the right decision. Nolan was a veteran coach with more than 20 years of experience. He was a defensive coordinator for seven different teams. He had been the head coach of the San Francisco 49ers. His father, Dick, was an NFL head coach with San Francisco and the New Orleans Saints and had also been an assistant coach with the Cowboys in the late 1960s and 1990s.

"I had an old coach tell me my first year when I was down and out and dejected in the dressing room over losing the games and only winning one game my first year with the Cowboys," Jerry Jones said in a 2017 radio interview. "This coach came over and said, 'Jerry, you've got to remember one thing: they pay their guys, too, on that side of the ball. You can get beat in the NFL.' So, consequently, when we step out there, we've got to remind ourselves that the wins are pressure, especially on the road."

That coach was Dick Nolan.

Jones respected the hire of Dick Nolan's son. The experience Jones wanted in a coaching staff was embraced. The last time

Nolan was a defensive coordinator was 2014 with the Atlanta Falcons. That year the Falcons finished last in the NFL in defense.

The global pandemic that closed the world forced coaches to conduct meetings virtually. Nolan was changing the defense from a four-man front to a three-man front. That's not a big deal, considering most if not all defenses in the NFL play out of a nickel defense consisting of four defensive linemen and three cornerbacks. But Nolan struggled to communicate with his players. Part of knowing football is explaining it to young and veteran NFL players.

The 2020 season would be different. The pandemic canceled on-the-field work in the offseason for NFL teams. Nolan couldn't get face-to-face meetings on a consistent basis to work his plan. The virtual world was like a new world to not only Nolan, but also many of the Cowboys' coaches This pandemic was turning traditional ways of teaching in person into old school. It seemed outdated. The way Nolan and his coaches wanted to educate the players seemed like the Stone Age. If Nolan had a plan of moving players into different positions, he couldn't see it on the practice field. It was a virtual world now. Nolan would need to visualize everything.

The Cowboys just couldn't help their players enough in changing the scheme. At one point during the 2020 season, Nolan made everything as simple as possible. "You look at just about everything obviously," Nolan said in the middle of October. "Your objective is to get better and the chemistry you need to build. Obviously, there's a lot of things here from culture to football, things like that. But my focus personally when it goes like it is now—and has been for a few weeks now—is just try to find ways to stimulate the growth as far as what we're doing. We've simplified all the way back to the very first game this season. So, it's not that we have too much volume in my opinion. I don't think players would say that either. It's really more of a case where we haven't played together. We haven't played very well at times in the games."

Today's NFL player is a visual performer. Present information is consumed via an iPad, cellphone, laptop, and they get it. The player of yesteryear needed meeting rooms with projection screens, chalk boards, or a computer to understand what was expected of him. Today's NFL player doesn't need that. Just show him a video. Just give him an iPhone. Just give him a tablet and get out of the way. Teaching became different, and if a coach or coaches couldn't adapt, he or she would get left behind. In fact, it would cost you games.

The Cowboys' defensive players liked Nolan as a person but not how he communicated. He just couldn't explain changes and why it mattered. When the season ended, the Cowboys record was 6–10, and the records set by opponents was an example of how bad this season was. In the big picture, losing Prescott after the fifth week of the regular season with a fractured right ankle was more damaging than anything. The defense didn't help matters. In some ways, it didn't help at all. The Cowboys defense allowed franchise records in points (473), touchdowns (54), and passing touchdowns (34).

Injuries at the cornerback position to projected starters, Jourdan Lewis, Trevon Diggs, and Chidobe Awuzie added to the issues of communication with Nolan. Defensive backs coach Maurice Linguist also failed to connect with pro players. He was mainly a college coach, and his ways didn't jive with veteran players. He needed to treat them like adults instead of a college player on scholarship. When the Cowboys had troubles at defensive back due to injuries, they brought in longtime Cowboys veteran Brandon Carr. Linguist and Carr clashed, and the cornerback's comeback ended after three games and 21 defensive snaps.

While the pandemic took a toll on America, it also wrecked how the NFL conducted its business. There were games with either few fans or none. The Cowboys were one of a handful of teams that hosted fans at AT&T Stadium in the beginning of the season. The Cowboys slowly increased the number of fans who attended games. When the season was over, the Cowboys led the NFL in attendance with 229,343 total fans. Groups of fans sat apart from each other, cash was no longer accepted, masks were required, and, ultimately, Jones, the team owner and general manager, cited the stadium's huge capacity with a terrific air flow and a comprehensive cleaning before, during, and after games that could make AT&T Stadium spotless. Safe. Jones felt it was a rite of passage to have fans watching football games. He wanted football, particularly the NFL, to help the country get out of its dizzy spell of the pandemic. A healing tool, if you will.

But watching Jones' football team during the 2020 season gave you no hope that McCarthy, in his first season on the job, was the right man for it. "Best talent of any team I've ever been around," McCarthy told Jones during the 2020 season.

How did he see this?

McCarthy signed a five-year contract to turn this franchise around. In year one McCarthy's team finished 6–10. There are no successes after a 6–10 season. None.

But there is learning, and McCarthy moved on from Nolan, firing the man once the season was over. It wasn't a difficult decision. It was a needed move, considering the communication issues Nolan had with several of his players. It even stretched to defensive line coach Jim Tomsula, another veteran coach, whose head wasn't in the game. These men meant well, but it was also an indictment of the coaching staff: it was poorly constructed.

Just before the end of the 2020 season, Dan Quinn, who was just fired after nearly six seasons in Atlanta as head coach, was mentioned as a replacement for Nolan. Quinn had previous success in the NFL as a defensive coordinator. He was the defensive coordinator with the Seattle Seahawks on the back end of the Legion of Boom era. That nickname was given to Seattle's dominant defense that employed standouts and future Hall of Fame players like cornerback Richard Sherman, safeties Earl Thomas and Kam Chancellor, and linebacker Bobby Wagner.

In Quinn's two seasons in charge of the defense, Seattle went to the Super Bowl. In 2013 Seattle was No. 1 in fewest yards and points allowed and most takeaways. Seattle crushed the Denver Broncos 43–8, picking off quarterback Peyton Manning twice and holding the running attack to just 27 yards. The next season, Seattle's defense again ranked No. 1 in yards and points and reached the Super Bowl. Instead of back-to-back titles, the Seahawks suffered a crushing loss to the New England Patriots 28–24 in Super Bowl XLIX. Quarterback Russell Wilson threw a back-breaking interception from the Patriots 1-yard line that sealed the win for New England.

Quinn left after that season to become a head coach in Atlanta.

His credentials were solidified by two strong seasons for a Seahawks defense with talented players. He didn't mess it up. So now he was asked to fix the Falcons defense. In nearly six seasons, Quinn compiled a 43–42 record, but as head coach, he underwent a heartbreaking loss, a loss his team never recovered from.

A New York Giants fan born in New Jersey who grew up with a Lawrence Taylor poster on his bedroom wall, Quinn understood hard-nosed defense. That's what he grew up watching in Jersey. Quinn had that in Seattle. He didn't have it totally in Atlanta. Yet, he led the Falcons to the Super Bowl and faced the Patriots again in Super Bowl LI. A 28–3 second-half lead gave the appearance of security. Just run the ball. Just get a few defensive stops, and Quinn would bring a championship to Atlanta. He would probably coach there forever. But the Patriots rallied and defeated the Falcons 34–28 in one of the great comebacks in NFL history.

Quinn would say years later you never get over it. "I have great memories there and I always will and I think a lot of the really cool things that we accomplished there—and there were a lot of them—versus how it ended," Quinn said. "That's an important declaration. I'll certainly be forever grateful to [Falcons owner] Arthur [Blank] to give me the opportunity there and to all of the players I had the privilege to coach."

NFL owners get over losses by firing coaches. And in 2020 Quinn was let go. So a potential marriage was possible between Quinn and the Cowboys. McCarthy, who sat out the 2019 season after getting fired himself in Green Bay, knew of Quinn. The relationship was of respect from afar. After Nolan's struggles and Quinn's availability, McCarthy hired Quinn.

When teams switch coordinators, especially on defense, personnel can change. Quinn wanted bigger players. He sought defensive linemen with long arms to push away from offensive linemen in pass protection. In the secondary he sought taller cornerbacks to deal with the taller receivers being selected each year in NFL drafts. Safeties and linebackers needed the abilities to make hard hits and in some cases work in pass coverage. "There would be some change as you're looking to do things," Quinn said. "I've been part of the same system for a good long time myself both in Seattle and Atlanta for that time. So I had some things that I wanted to change as well—certainly, a combination of things, the foundation that has been here, as well as some new things that I wanted to bring into it and how we play and the style that would do that."

The other component, something Nolan was unable to have, was on-the-field work. The NFL struggled to work within the pandemic. Not in 2021. NFL teams got back on the practice fields, and if any scheme change was going to happen, it would make it easier for coaches and players to understand each other. In late March Cowboys linebacker Jaylon Smith said of Quinn, "[In 2020] around this time, we were dealing with COVID and all of that good stuff, so really being able to take advantage of learning the true details of what we need to do to accomplish and be a successful defense [is important]."

Said veteran defensive end Randy Gregory of Quinn's approach: "He's got a lot of one-liners and a lot of phrases. He put a bunch of papers up on the wall that say priority and all of the things that we consider a priority as a defense…I think a lot of guys, as far as defense goes, really respond to that—something that we can [think] back on when times get rough out there on the field, definitely want that type of guy to push you on as a defense."

Quinn was given the power in free agency to get players he wanted. Keanu Neal, a safety turned linebacker, signed as a free agent to compete for playing time with Leighton Vander Esch and Smith. Safety Damontae Kazee was also signed in free agency. Both players signed one-year deals and were coming off torn Achilles injuries. Safety Jayron Kearse was also signed in free agency. Quinn envisioned Kearse covering tight ends in pass coverage because of his 6'4", 215-pound frame. The only problem was Kearse was mainly a special teams player while playing for two teams, the Minnesota Viking and Detroit Lions, in a five-year career. In sports, mainly the NFL, these one-year deals are called "prove it deals." If Kearse, Kazee, and Neal provided the Cowboys with solid play during the 2021 season, then it was quite possible they would get another contract with the Cowboys or elsewhere. NFL players want stability, and their play on the field dictates that more than anything.

Quinn needed to fix the secondary, and the Cowboys needed a cornerback desperately. It'd been years since this team had one of quality. Going into the 2021 NFL Draft, the veteran starters were Anthony Brown and Diggs. Replacing Diggs wasn't happening. He was a 2020 second-round pick, a player the team almost traded up for but instead stayed put to select him 51st overall. The Cowboys had a first-round grade on Diggs and to find him in the second round of the 2020 NFL Draft was a present it didn't expect.

Diggs was a starter. But you need three or four cornerbacks in the pass-happy NFL.

Brown was someone for whom the Cowboys wanted to create competition. He wasn't elite but serviceable given what the NFL is now. Cornerbacks could be elite in college, but the NFL was a different animal. This was a draft in which the Cowboys coveted one. After their 6–10 season, the Cowboys owned the No. 10 overall pick. Given their top 10 draft position, there were two cornerbacks worth looking at. Jaycee Horn from South

Carolina and Alabama's Patrick Surtain II were considered the best corners in the draft. The Cowboys were poised to get one.

Both players came from NFL stock. Surtain's father, Patrick Surtain, played 11 years in the NFL. He was a three-time Pro Bowler with one All-Pro season. During his time in the NFL, he had 37 career interceptions. He knows about the cornerback position. His son was born to it.

Jaycee Horn's dad, Joe, was a wide receiver in the National Football League. Joe Horn played for three teams during a 12-year career. Horn, like Surtain, raised a son to play in the NFL.

So two players at the top of draft boards were going to get drafted by cornerback-needy teams. Perfect.

The best cornerbacks in the history of the Cowboys are Mel Renfro, Everson Walls, and Deion Sanders. Renfro and Walls were homegrown. Renfro was a second-round pick and finished his career as a Hall of Famer with 10 Pro Bowl berths. Walls was an undrafted free agent from Grambling. He went to four Pro Bowls. One of the missing pieces to the late title runs in the 1990s, Sanders signed with the Cowboys as a free agent. Terence Newman and Mike Jenkins were former first-round picks that had an impact. Orlando Scandrick, a fifth-round pick, is another corner who played well for the Cowboys.

But finding one for the future is where the Cowboys resided now. "We've got a good chance to have a top defensive player. The top, or one of the top, [should] be there at 10," Jerry Jones said the night before the NFL draft. "I know from the past that when you start talking about being where there is one of the top, whether it be at a position or on one side of the ball or the other, there is a lot of action that can happen there. You can get a lot of phone calls. If that phone is not ringing, that is them not calling, so to speak."

The issue was who to select.

Quinn liked Horn's size at 6'1", 200 pounds, but a defensive coordinator from another NFL team had this assessment of him: "Horn is physical, sometimes to a fault."

Some scouts believed Horn didn't know how to control his body in a way to make plays on the ball. He was too wild, scouts would say. At South Carolina, Horn had 23 career pass breakups.

That same defensive coordinator said of Surtain: "He's more technically sound."

A consensus had Surtain as the safe pick and why not. Surtain had 24 pass breakups with four interceptions over three seasons at Alabama. Surtain was 6'2" and 208 pounds, and the Cowboys had him ranked higher on their board. He was the target. The Cowboys scouts and coaches virtually met with both players. The conversations were considered positive. There was a split in the organization on who was better, but it wasn't a wide divide.

Though many around the NFL figured the Cowboys would select a corner in the first round, there was someone else making noise: Micah Parsons from Penn State. The linebacker from Harrisburg, Pennsylvania, was a tremendous talent. He missed the 2020 season, opting out due to the coronavirus and to prepare for the NFL draft. In two seasons consisting of 26 games, Parsons had 191 tackles, 18 tackles for loss, and 6.5 sacks.

The final game of the 2019 season for Penn State was against Memphis in the Cotton Bowl played at AT&T Stadium. Parsons was magnificent. The sophomore had 14 tackles, three tackles for loss, two forced fumbles, two sacks, and two pass breakups.

He also forced an interception on a quarterback hurry. He was named the Cotton Bowl's Outstanding Defensive Player. "This is where I wanted to be," Parsons said of playing at AT&T Stadium. "I wanted to play here; I wanted to be in this blue and white until I die. It felt like home when I was here for the Memphis game."

If this was a way to finish a career, then so be it. The awards came in strong for Parsons. He was named a consensus All-American by the NCAA, Associated Press, and *USA TODAY*.

Parsons' decision to leave after two college seasons was difficult. The lure of the NFL for star players is great, especially for one of his abilities. Plus, Parsons had a child named Malcolm who he wanted to provide for. "When you have a son, your whole world changes," Parsons said in an interview with Penn Live in August 2020. "I really thought about him because as I was growing up I was in Harrisburg and I never really had much. And now I look at this great opportunity for me to work hard and me to really give him the life that I never had. It's so hard for me to pass it up."

Parsons thought about returning for the 2020 season. The emotions of wanting to play with teammates and for head coach James Franklin again were great. But Parsons elected to stay away. He would focus on the NFL draft. This decision was about family—not his college teammates. If NFL teams had questions about Parsons, his Pro Day at Penn State answered everything. He ran a 4.39 40-yard dash, displaying the speed NFL scouts saw during games. The fastest time set by a linebacker at the NFL Scouting Combine was 4.38 set by Shaquem Griffin in 2018. Parsons beat that. Parsons also benched pressed 225 pounds 19 times and produced a 34-inch vertical leap. The speed, power, and ability to move laterally resulted in extremely high marks for the linebacker. So did his versatility. "I can play middle line-backer, I can play outside, and I can pass rush," Parsons said. "I don't think there's no place I can't play in a linebacker spot."

There was one major issue with Parsons; he was mentioned in a lawsuit against Penn State for a 2018 hazing incident with a teammate. The lawsuit contended Parsons threw cold water on teammate Isaiah Humphries while he was sleeping. The two got into a fistfight with Humphries pulling a knife on Parsons. Humphries' lawsuit said several other teammates hazed him with graphic details of several incidents, including simulated sex, vulgar language, and other types of verbal humiliation. Parsons was eventually cleared of wrongdoing, yet character issues arose because of it.

Draft guides treated Parsons much differently in comparison to other players with off-the-field problems. This is how The Athletic described Alabama quarterback Mac Jones' off-the-field issue in its draft guide: "Scouts love his character, but he was arrested and charged for DUI and a fake driver ID [November 2017] during his redshirt season...only 17 career starts on his resume."

This is how they described Parsons: "During the fall of his junior year, he was suspended for an incident in the school cafeteria. He transferred midseason to Harrisburg High School [October 2016] due to his mother moving out of the district [they moved in with his grandparents]. Parsons was accused in a civil lawsuit against Penn State of participating in hazing incidents against former teammate Isaiah Humphries. Parsons was not named as a defendant in the suit. Parsons elected to opt out of playing last season and declared for the NFL draft...maturity concerns have been attached to him in high school and college, although Penn

State coaches have stuck up for him. [Penn State head coach James Franklin: '99.9 percent of the time, he's been good']…missed one start as a sophomore with a 'behavioral' issue [November 2019]… only one season as a full-time starter."

It seemed extreme that a draft guide would go into high school to discuss a prospective draft pick's behavior. A player transferring from one school to another in high school being mentioned in a draft guide raises questions about how deep a player's background should be reviewed. The notes would also indicate somebody was leaking information to draft experts, and

Defensive Rookie of the Year Micah Parsons takes down Kansas City Chiefs quarterback Patrick Mahomes for one of his two sacks in the Week 11 game.

NFL teams were also getting the same information. But could it be used against you?

NFL teams take players off their draft boards if they believe a prospective player is going to be a long-term problem. Parsons was not that. Yet a hazing incident was given significant play with draft experts and some teams. There were numerous media reports about whether Parsons behavior was an issue for NFL teams.

Quinn didn't care. The Cowboys didn't either. Of course, they did the necessary homework on Parsons. They spoke with Coach Franklin, all the necessary assistant coaches, and support staff to get a true picture of Parsons. Quinn loved what he could do with Parsons. He saw him as a middle linebacker that would compete with veterans Vander Esch and Smith. Quinn had detailed conversations with him during the draft. "It was very interesting," Parsons said. "He was talking about all the things he liked on my tape and he was going to send me on a lot of blitzes and have me man a lot of backs and tight ends, and I'm going to match up well with a bunch of good running backs in our division. I'm excited to do that for him and compete at a high level."

But the Cowboys needed a cornerback.

Parsons was a player that might be available when it was time for the Cowboys to draft with the No. 10 overall pick. And Parsons told family and friends he wanted to play for the Cowboys. He dreamed it would happen. Playing in the Cotton Bowl gave him a sense of peace that he belonged at AT&T Stadium. The Cowboys had other ideas on draft night. When the first round began, the Cowboys would know quickly about which defensive player they would acquire. Detroit took offensive tackle Penei Sewell with the seventh overall pick, and that's when the fun started.

The Carolina Panthers were at No. 8. There were rumors of the Panthers selecting a quarterback. Yet, the Panthers had traded with the New York Jets for Sam Darnold and picked up his fifth-year option. Darnold was going to be QB1 at least for the next season. Three quarterbacks were already off the board. Ohio State's Justin Fields and Alabama's Jones were available.

The Panthers snagged Horn with the eighth overall pick. He became the first defensive player off the board. So now it was time for the Broncos. Dallas' main player was sitting there in Surtain. Should Dallas at the No. 10 spot try to trade with Denver?

If anything, the Cowboys thought about moving up to No. 6 with the Miami Dolphins. There was a chance Horn and Surtain would be off the board by the time No. 10 came around. "We didn't want to give up what it would take to get up there," Stephen Jones said.

So at No. 9 Denver took Surtain. And that meant the two best corners on the Cowboys' draft board were gone.

The Cowboys were on the clock now, and the New York Giants and Philadelphia Eagles followed at No. 11 and No. 12, respectively. "We were sitting there at 10 and we didn't want to go too far back because we really liked Micah and we didn't want to get in a position where we didn't think we could get him," Stephen Jones said. "Philly had called—and with what they were trying to do—it was obvious they were trying to get in front of the Giants and get the player they were after. We really felt like we knew what they were going to take. They told us what side of the ball [they were drafting]. We felt like we would get through the Giants and still get our player and pick up a third-round pick."

The Eagles offered a third-round pick to the Cowboys to switch spots. The Cowboys weren't afraid that Parsons, who also thought the Giants had a strong interest in him, would get picked before their turn. Parsons' close friend and Penn State alum Saquon Barkley played for the Giants. During the preparation of the draft, Parsons worked out with Barkley in California. Playing with his close friend in New York was a big desire. "You are looking for the value there," Jones said. "That wasn't a hesitation. You may have three or four other considerations there and you are looking to get the most value for the pick. At the same time, we had our eye on Micah and didn't want to get too far down that road."

The Eagles had made a trade earlier in the night, moving from No. 6 to No. 12 with Miami in addition to giving up a fifth-round pick in 2021. Also, the Dolphins gave up a fourth-round selection and a 2022 first-round pick. "When we made the trade from six to 12, we really had to make a list of guys that we would have been really happy to take at 12," Eagles executive vice president/general manager Howie Roseman said. "From March to Draft Day, a lot has changed. I think at the time maybe we thought there would be more quarterbacks, to be honest with you, going before we picked. And at the same time, we also had a projection of what would go in front of us."

After the trade with the Cowboys, the Eagles took Alabama wide receiver DeVonta Smith at No. 10. Now the Giants were on the clock. The possibility of Parsons going to the Giants wasn't real. Stephen Jones knew the Giants were going to trade down. Any fears the Giants wanted Parsons were faint. However, the Chicago Bears, needing a quarterback, traded with the Giants, moving from No. 20 to No. 11 to select Ohio State's Fields.

Dallas was on the clock.

Parsons was ranked higher than the two cornerbacks the Cowboys failed to obtain, and moving up took too much draft capital to get them. Parsons sat in a green room inside Cleveland's FirstEnergy Stadium wearing a blue double-breasted suit with a black turtleneck. Family and friends stood around him waiting for one of his two cellphones to ring. "Hello," Parsons said, holding one of the phones with his right hand.

Jerry Jones was welcoming Parsons to the Cowboys. Parsons' family began to scream. "Yes, sir," Parsons said as he put his hands over his eyes. "This is all I ever wanted, man."

Parsons bit his bottom lip, trying to control his emotions. It was difficult. Parsons' son, Malcolm, hugged his dad. "Let's Go!" a family member screamed.

"We going to Texas," another said.

"It was meant to be," someone said.

Parsons hung up and hugged some family members. Of course, the selection was made before it's officially announced on television. The entire Parsons family stood watching a flat-screen television broadcasting the draft. Parsons was in front waiting for his name to be called.

While it's official with the Cowboys turning Parsons name into the league office, waiting for the announcement makes it *official official.*

When Micah Parsons told his father, Terrence Parsons Sr., he was going to play in the NFL, few believed it. Micah Parsons believed this opportunity is a prophecy because his mother, Sherese, had him when she was 24 and thought about aborting the pregnancy because she was too young and had two other kids. In an interview with PennLive, Sherese said a woman from a church called her in the wee hours of the night and told her, "Have your baby. You don't know what you're giving up."

Sherese and Terrence sacrificed to make it work with three kids with the hope things would get better. And now here was Micah Parsons, the baby, the youngest of three, living out his dream of becoming an NFL player. The announcement was made, and the Parsons family jumped up and down with excitement. "Yeah, I spoke it into existence. Words have a lot of power," Parsons said. "If you believe in something, you're going to achieve something if you put your mind to it. I probably had a 10 percent chance of this ever happening, but all I need is a percent."

Parsons left his family to take a walk to meet NFL commissioner Roger Goodell. Every first-round pick in Goodell's tenure meets with him on a big stage. In 2020 Goodell couldn't do that. He had to do it virtually because of the pandemic, but by 2021 the restrictions the country was under were more relaxed. Here was Parsons taking a walk alone, the last one he would have as a college player. He was becoming a pro football player now.

He underwent the scrutiny of his character, even though he had grades that allowed him to leave high school early so he could enroll at Penn State sooner. He picked up his degree in criminology in three years. He did everything early to get ready for something bigger. "Obviously, false allegations and how the media portrays them sometimes without really a deep dive into the truth," Parsons said, "the truth always comes to light, and the Cowboys did their job in digging into [it]. They know I am a high-character player and person."

Parsons was handed a black cap with the Cowboys draft logo sitting above the bill. He saw a smiling Goodell and jumped in his arms. Parsons cried. Goodell smiled. And the Cowboys got their linebacker of the future. "It's hard not to see him, when you watch him play, to be that strong, that fast, that physical, and that instinctive," said Will McClay, the Cowboys vice president of player personnel. "When [Penn State] played out here at the Cotton Bowl and you see him out here you say, 'Oh. That's something,' because you don't see guys that big, that fast, and that athletic. Then getting to know him and his intensity level and his desire to be great, that was the thing that stood out the most when we got to talking. You can see what he does out on the field, but then you get to find out more about the young man and about what he can bring to you. I think that was the most attractive thing."

Quinn believed in Parsons. He saw it at Penn State's Pro Day. He saw the speed, the power, and the attitude needed to play linebacker. Quinn had a plan for Parsons. He didn't know if he was going to get him. Quinn would have been happy with one of the top cornerbacks to create more competition there. But through trades and conversations on a Thursday night in April, the Cowboys traded down from No. 10 to No. 12 to select Parsons.

Sometimes a draft is about luck. Sometimes a draft is about staying true to the board. The Cowboys had both. There was no need to reach for a player that wasn't going to benefit you in the long run. In 2020 the Cowboys did this by staying true to their board and getting Oklahoma wide receiver CeeDee Lamb when they needed a defensive player in the first round. Lamb was a highly-regarded player and the highest-ranked player on the Cowboys board when they picked him at 17th overall.

Believing in the scouts and personnel people is vital during a draft. Media and fans like to believe Jerry Jones is just throwing darts on a board when it comes to picking players. He does have the final say, but he listens. He watches. He reads. He studies. He understands. He believes in his staff. The staff believed in trading down, so that's what he did, even though it was with a division rival like the Eagles.

It was a gamble. "The first part about us trading up is obviously the more you trade up in the round, the more you're going to have to give up," Roseman said of the trade. "By the same token, when you trade in the division, you understand that you're not going to get any values to that either. It's going to have to work for them as well."

Jones was told Parsons would be available. He believed in it. It happened. Despite growing up in Eagles country, Parsons and his family were big Cowboys fans. To reach this stage, Parsons had to wait. He sat out the 2020 season when playing would have benefited him. He let his two seasons at Penn State do the talking for him. "It was a very tough decision," Parsons said. "I had to sit down with my family multiple times and I had a lot of mentors that I met throughout my process like [former Penn State and NFL star] LaVar [Arrington] and some past linebackers that came through the NFL. I don't think I'm making up time. I think I'm right on time. I'm right where I need to be, and as soon as I get here, we're gonna get right to work and become a better football team."

Parsons hung out in Arrington's home in Southern California, and the two spoke about the pressures of playing in the NFL. Arrington, the second overall pick of the then-Washington Redskins in 2000, knows about the expectations of being a high draft pick and trying to succeed. Arrington, a Penn State alum who also played linebacker, wore the same jersey number as Parsons. He didn't just let anybody in his inner circle. Arrington said that circle is tight, but once someone is in, he or she was in. Parsons was in. The two developed such a close bond that when Arrington left his house to attend to business, he trusted Parsons to stay there.

Parsons talked to many about his draft journey. It was important for him to get it correct. He sat out the 2020 season for a reason. It was for his son, his family, and for his football future. The draft journey was going to be difficult, but he needed to perform well at his Pro Day, which he did, and say the right things to NFL teams. He had worked out in front of Quinn at his Pro Day and had one virtual call with the Cowboys. Jerry Jones wasn't on the call that day. It wouldn't matter in the big picture of things because Jones was getting the reports of a talented player who could be coming into his organization.

So when the Parsons family arrived in Cleveland, Ohio, for the draft, the team he dreamed of going to was looking at a cornerback. As everything unfolded, two corners were taken. Although the Cowboys say they weren't surprised by that, it was still a jolt for their original plan of getting a defensive back. It worked out well for all parties. "I'm happy for them," Parsons said. "I train with Jaycee, and Pat has been my boy since high school. Nothing but happiness for those guys. What was going through my mind was that it was going to be my turn soon, so I was thinking that."

Parsons' dream was complete. He was a Dallas Cowboy. It's something he aspired for after he first played in AT&T Stadium as a collegiate in the Cotton Bowl. "Just think if you were 21 years old and you just met Jerry Jones," he said. "It's pretty freaking awesome."

Parsons called himself the "Lion." His rookie season was sensational. Although the Cowboys didn't draft the cornerback they sought, trading down with the Eagles gave them a chance to draft Parsons. The 2021 season was The Year of the Lion. Parsons had a stretch where he recorded a sack in six consecutive games. When the 2021 year concluded, Parsons had played outside linebacker, defensive end, and middle linebacker, creating a positionless role for himself the Cowboys hope to use for years to come.

ACKNOWLEDGMENTS

WHEN I STARTED this project, I was scared. Most writers want to write a book but don't understand the time it takes.

I just want to thank a few people, starting with Marcus Thompson, who was one of the first people I called. He told me about the blood he left on his living room and bedroom floors just from writing. I want to thank him for being real with me about the book. Just write, he said, because you already know what to say. He was right. Watching Bob Glauber and Jarrett Bell finish their own projects was a tremendous inspiration for me. They probably didn't know I was watching, but I was. Jean-Jacques Taylor and Clarence Hill were more than friends to me. The support they gave me is something I will never forget.

Everyone at Triumph Books was patient with me, and I can't thank them enough. I was humbled they thought of me to write this and remain that way now after its completion. Also, my people at *The Dallas Morning News*, you allowed me to write this, and I'm forever grateful.

Being a sportswriter is a job of inconvenience. You love the job because, well, we're covering sporting events and not serving coffee, flipping burgers, or asking what type of cigar you like. Nothing wrong with those types of jobs, but to watch men and women play sports and to write about it is a dream job.

When I was approached about writing a book, I thought it was another dream. How could someone think of me about writing a book? Maybe I've undervalued my worth as a sportswriter. Maybe I've taken this job for granted. But I'm grateful for the opportunity to finish this project.

Also there are so many people involved when it comes to getting drafted in the National Football League. I appreciate all of you telling your stories whether it was to me or someone else. The dream of playing in the NFL is something no one can take away from you, and getting drafted is just part of that. I'm glad your dreams have come true.

My wife, Cindy, and three kids, Myles, Rome, and Shalon, remind me I'm living out my own dream.

I finally want to thank my wife, Cindy. She scares me. Every time I wasn't writing something, I was afraid to tell her. She was my coach. She was my general manager. She was my everything. Without her push this book would have failed. But it succeeded. Thank you.